Entrepreneurs and the Search for the American Dream

This book's central focus explores several "myths" associated with American entrepreneurship: the idea that small business owners are "job creators"; that entrepreneurs are the "backbone" or "engine" of the economy; that entrepreneurship provides a path of economic mobility for immigrants, ethnic and racial minorities, and women; that the Horatio Algiers "rags to riches" story is possible for anyone willing to work hard. Instead, this book provides a critical perspective that challenges these myths of American enterprise, arguing that successful entrepreneurship requires access to social and economic capital resources and support that are often distributed along the lines of race, class, and gender in the highly stratified American economy and society.

Zulema Valdez is Associate Professor of Sociology at the University of California, Merced. Her interests include intersectionality, Latino/a sociology, and social inequality. She is the author of *The New Entrepreneurs: How Race, Class and Gender Shape American Enterprise* (2011).

Framing Twenty-first Century Social Issues

Series Editor: France Winddance Twine, University of California, Santa Barbara

The goal of this new, unique series is to offer readable, teachable "thinking frames" on today's social problems and social issues by leading scholars. These are available for view on http://routledge.customgateway.com/routledge-social-issues.html.

For instructors teaching a wide range of courses in the social sciences, the Routledge *Social Issues Collection* now offers the best of both worlds: originally written short texts that provide "overviews" to important social issues *as well as* teachable excerpts from larger works previously published by Routledge and other presses.

As an instructor, click to the website to view the library and decide how to build your custom anthology and which thinking frames to assign. Students can choose to receive the assigned materials in print and/or electronic formats at an affordable price.

Available:

The Global Beauty Industry
Colorism, Racism, and the National Body
Meeta Rani Jha

Outsourcing the Womb, Second Edition
Race, Class, and Gestational Surrogacy in a Global Market
France Winddance Twine

Confronting Campus Rape
Legal Landscapes, New Media, and Networked Activism
Danielle Dirks

Oversharing, Second Edition
Presentation of Self in the Internet Age
Ben Agger

Social Problems
A Human Rights Perspective
Eric Bonds

The Enduring Color Line in U.S. Athletics
Krystal Beamon and Chris M. Messer

Identity Problems in the Facebook Era
Daniel Trottier

The Pains of Mass Imprisonment
Benjamin Fleury-Steiner and Jamie G. Longazel

From Trafficking to Terror
Constructing a Global Social Problem
Pardis Mahdavi

Unequal Prospects
Is Working Longer the Answer?
Tay McNamara and John Williamson

Beyond the Prison Industrial Complex
Crime and Incarceration in the Twenty-first Century
Kevin Wehr and Elyshia Aseltine

Girls with Guns
Firearms, Feminism, and Militarism
France Winddance Twine

Terror
Social, Political, and Economic Perspectives
Mark Worrell

Torture
A Sociology of Violence and Human Rights
Lisa Hajjar

Entrepreneurs and the Search for the American Dream

Zulema Valdez

Routledge
Taylor & Francis Group

NEW YORK AND LONDON

First published 2016
by Routledge
711 Third Avenue, New York, NY 10017

and by Routledge
2 Park Square, Milton Park, Abingdon, Oxon, OX14 4RN

Routledge is an imprint of the Taylor & Francis Group, an informa business

Library of Congress Cataloging-in-Publication Data
Valdez, Zulema.
   Entrepreneurs and the search for the American dream/Zulema Valdez.
   pages cm.—(Framing 21st century social issues)
   Includes bibliographical references and index.
   1. Entrepreneurship—United States. 2. Businesspeople—United States.
   3. Social mobility—United States. I. Title.
   HB615.V3484 2016
   338′.040973—dc23
   2015022711

ISBN: 978-1-138-64859-3 (hbk)
ISBN: 978-1-138-92255-6 (pbk)
ISBN: 978-1-315-68581-6 (ebk)

Typeset in Adobe Garamond and Gill Sans
by Florence Production Ltd, Stoodleigh, Devon, UK

Contents

Series Foreword

The first decades of the twenty-first century have been a time of paradoxes. Growing prosperity and the growth of the middle classes in countries such as Brazil, China, India, Russia, and South Africa have been accompanied by climate change, environmental degradation, labor exploitation, sexual abuse, and sexual violence targeting girls and women, state censorship of social media, governmental corruption, and human rights abuses. Sociologists offer theories, concepts and analytical frames that enable us to better understand the challenges and cultural transformations of the twenty-first century. How can we generate new forms of collective knowledge that can help solve some of our local, global, and transnational problems?

We live in a world in which new communication technologies and products such as mobile cellular phones, iPads, and new social media such as Facebook, Google, Skype, and Twitter have transformed on-line education, global communication networks, local and transnational economies, facilitated revolutions such as the "Arab Spring," and generated new forms of entertainment, employment, protest, and pleasure. These social media have been utilized by social justice activists, political dissidents, educators, entrepreneurs, and multinational corporations. They have also been a resource employed to facilitate corporate deviance, government corruption, and the increased surveillance of civilian populations. This form of use threatens democracy, privacy, creative expression, and political freedoms.

This is the fifth year of our Routledge Twenty-first Century Social Issues Series. Our series includes books on topics ranging broadly from climate change, consumption, eugenics, torture, sports, medical technologies, gun violence, the internet, and youth culture. These books explore contemporary social problems in ways that introduce basic sociological concepts in the social sciences, cover key literature in the field, and offer original diagnoses. They also engage directly in current debates within the social sciences over how to best define, rethink, and respond to the social concerns that preoccupy the early twenty-first century.

The goal of this series is to provide accessible essays that examine a wide range of social issues whose impacts are local, global, and transnational. Sociologists are ideally poised to contribute to a global conversation about a range of issues such as the impact of mass incarceration on local economies, medical technologies, health disparities, violence, torture, transnational migration, militarism, and the AIDS epidemic. The contributors to this series bring together the works of classical sociology into dialogue with contemporary social theorists from diverse theoretical traditions including but not limited to feminist, Marxist, and European social theory.

Readers do not need an extensive background in academic sociology to benefit from these books. Each book is student-friendly in that we provide glossaries of terms for the uninitiated that are keyed to bolded terms in the text. Each chapter ends with questions for further thought and discussion. The level of each book is ideal for undergraduates because they are accessible without sacrificing a theoretically sophisticated and innovative analysis.

Zulema Valdez provides us with an original, innovative, and much-needed analysis of the ways that the ideology of the American Dream conceals the real experiences of a diverse group of entrepreneurs who struggle and often fail to sustain their small businesses. We learn from Valdez how the ideology of the American Dream and the dominant discourse that through hard work everyone can achieve this actually conceals the ongoing forms of social inequality, gender inequality, and the divisions within ethnic communities. In other words, Valdez forces us to have a more nuanced analysis of a complex situation that often leads to failures as much as success. For anyone interested in how working people survive and negotiate being business owners in an oppressive system, this book lifts the curtain to show the real landscape of entrepreneurship for those who fall outside of the Dream. This book offers a clearly written and critical analysis of the ways that race, class, gender, ethnicity, and migration status can simultaneously expand and restrict the opportunities available to entrepreneurs. This book will inspire the reader to rethink their beliefs about the American Dream and small business owners. This is an ideal book for courses on race and ethnicity, social inequality, race/class/gender, economic sociology, and American Studies.

France Winddance Twine
Series Editor

Preface

Entrepreneurs and the Search for the American Dream seeks to examine the divergent life chances of American entrepreneurs from a perspective that addresses the ways that race, ethnicity, class, and gender are intertwined and interact. Many social scientists consider the role of race *or* gender *or* class in shaping the opportunities and outcomes of entrepreneurs in the United States. This book introduces an intersectional approach to the study of entrepreneurship that gives attention to multiple and intersecting forms of inequality, or what sociologists call "stratification."

The book demonstrates that these distinct yet interdependent social groupings affect whether or to what extent entrepreneurs will fail, falter, surpass, or achieve the American Dream. It also reveals that these diverse dimensions of status, identity, and group membership structure the ideas, discourses, and symbolic meanings of the American Dream. What is the American Dream? Why do U.S. entrepreneurs of diverse ethnic backgrounds believe that they have "made it," regardless of whether they are barely surviving or thriving beyond all expectation?

In the United States, which remains a highly stratified society, entrepreneurs are unequally positioned and must navigate multiple hierarchies including age, class, ethnicity, race, gender, and region, which determine their unequal starting position in the social structure. Inequalities at the starting gate almost always contribute to unequal economic outcomes. The book reveals that the American Dream of business ownership and economic success remains out of reach for most. Nevertheless, it also demonstrates that entrepreneurship may provide a crucial and viable alternative to labor market uncertainty, including joblessness, racial or religious discrimination, or employer abuse and exploitation.

Ultimately, this book responds to and challenges an earlier body of literature in which the orthodox analytical approach to understanding entrepreneurship has been to focus on either white, middle class, and male "rugged individualists" who achieve success through determination and innovation, or "ethnic entrepreneurs" who rely on ethnic ties and collectivist ideologies to gain a foothold in business, thereby avoiding discrimination in the general labor market. Instead, I consider how individual agency, group membership, and structural forces shape American enterprise. I argue that the intersection of race, class, gender, and other social groupings, condition entrepreneurial experiences and outcomes in the highly stratified American economy. Overall, the cases in this book reveal how agency and structure as integrative forces reflect, reshape, and reproduce the hierarchically ranked American economy and society and how multiple and intersecting identities rooted in race, class, and gender contribute differently to entrepreneurs' social and economic progress.

Finally, the book offers a corrective to the strong belief held by most Americans that entrepreneurship is always a net positive for the economy and society. It challenges several myths about the relationship between entrepreneurship and the economy, including the myth that anyone who is willing to work hard can succeed in enterprise, that small businesses are the "engines of the economy," and that business owners are "job creators" with the power to stimulate growth during economic downturns. By considering the intersection of multiple dimensions of identity, within the context of an unequal and stratified economy, this book reveals how individual agency, group dynamics, and structural forces combine to shape, transform, and reproduce the divergent life chances of American entrepreneurs, and ultimately, their potential to achieve the American Dream.

Acknowledgements

I thank the entrepreneurs who shared their stories and never give up. I offer a special thank you to France Winddance Twine for her friendship and support, and for giving me the chance to write this book. I thank my friends, mentors, and family members for helping me through the process of writing and thinking, and for providing an unending source of inspiration and strength: Tanya Golash-Boza, Nitasha Sharma, Neha Vora, Vanita Reddy, Cara Wallis, and Andrew Yinger.

1:   Who Is an Entrepreneur and What Is Entrepreneurship?

~~~

"Risk more than others think is safe. Dream more than others think is practical."

Howard Schultz, CEO of Starbucks

Who Is an Entrepreneur?

Social scientists, politicians, journalists, and even entrepreneurs, describe entrepreneurs differently. When broadly defined, entrepreneurs may include self-employed workers—people who work on their own account with no paid employees—small business owners who work for themselves and hire others, and business owners who create large companies with thousands of employees. Some studies attempt to distinguish explicitly the entrepreneur from the small business owner. Schumpeter (1934), a German economist and political scientist and the most prominent scholar in the field of entrepreneurship, stated that the principle goals of the entrepreneur are to innovate and make a profit. In contrast, he described the small business owner as one who is driven by personal goals, whose business is a source of income that is "intricately bound with individual and family needs and desires."

If we accept the Schumpeterian definition, entrepreneurs are creators who bring new ideas to the market, develop new products or provide new services, and seek to maximize profits and grow their businesses. This conception, however, tends to exclude most self-employed workers or small business owners, whose businesses do not require a new discovery and whose owners may not pursue opportunities for economic advancement beyond achieving some measure of household economic security. Moreover, this distinction may appear at first glance to differentiate entrepreneurs from non-entrepreneurs; yet it does not capture small businesses and their owners that are entrepreneurial-like, for example, those businesses that outperform the owner's initial expectations or entrepreneurs who innovate on the margins such as Lorraine Santoli, the creator of TissueKups Inc. Her product dispenses tissues out of a cup, which fit in most vehicle cup holders; yet, tissues, cups, and cup holders in cars existed well before she combined them in a "new" way (Baron and Shane 2007: 3). It also fails to capture those would-be entrepreneurs with dreams to expand, but who fall short. As David Ogilvy, co-founder of Ogilvy & Mather, one of the largest advertising companies in the world, succinctly put it, "In the modern world of business, it is useless to be a creative, original thinker unless you can also sell what you create." Is an aspirational small business owner who is unable to expand an entrepreneur?

Furthermore, conceptualizing (non-entrepreneurial) small business owners as those who are engaged in ordinary or unoriginal enterprises with limited ambitions may correspond with most Americans' notion of the typical mom and pop shop around the corner or the family-owned restaurant down the street; however, it does not fit in neatly with the standard definition used by the U.S. government's Small Business Administration (SBA). The SBA defines a **small business** using a combination of measures including employee size, industry classification, and average receipts, and this generally includes manufacturing businesses with less than 500 employees and nonmanufacturing businesses that generate less than $7.5 million in annual receipts. As Figure 1.1 shows, *99.7 percent of all U.S. firms fall under this*

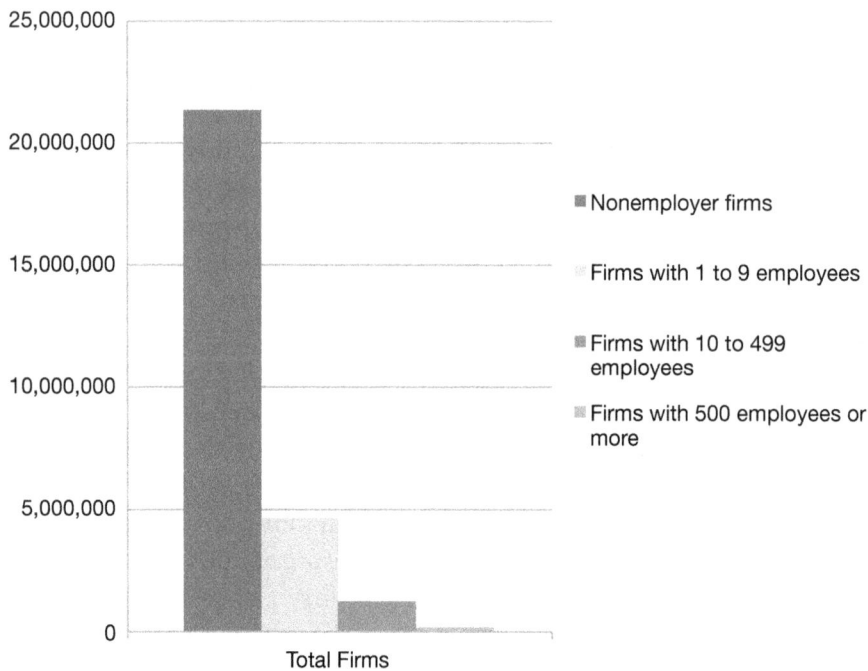

Figure 1.1 Nonemployer and Employer Firms by Employee Size

broad classification, which not much includes the typical mom and pop shop, but also much larger firms with hundred of employees that generate millions of dollars.

Given that the vast majority of American businesses fall under this definition of "small," it is not surprising that the SBA standard is inconsistently applied by the government. For example, the newly introduced Affordable Care Act (ACA), also known as ObamaCare, uses a different threshold to determine small businesses. The ACA states, "small businesses with the equivalent of less than 25 full-time workers, making less than $50,000 in average annual wages," qualify for tax breaks and credits. These subsidies are not available to larger businesses. For example, businesses with fifty full-time workers must offer health insurance to all full-time workers or pay a penalty. The different size classifications offered by the ACA suggest that the SBA definition of small (those with up to 499 employees) is too big. Moreover, this classification of small business dwarfs those used by other industrialized countries. For example, the European Union defines small business firms as those with fewer than fifty employees, or a tenth of that of the United States, whereas Canada considers small employer businesses to have between one and ninety-nine employees only (Europa 2015).

Finally, accepting Schumpeter's (1934) distinction between entrepreneurs and small business owners requires disregarding the two ubiquitous reasons for starting businesses given by the vast majority of business owners, regardless of creativity, growth, or firm size: to earn more money and be their own boss (Valdez 2011). Not only do these two key motivations consistently forecast entry into business ownership; they also predict whether business owners stay in business over the long term.

Instead of focusing on motivations, some researchers classify entrepreneurs by their individual characteristics and features. This line of reasoning tends to make tacit claims about the traits, skills, attitudes, and values that entrepreneurs share in common, and which separate them from employees. For example, entrepreneurs are often described as possessing characteristics that encourage business ownership, including being hard-working, risk-taking, optimistic, creative, and perhaps less positive but still somewhat desirable traits such as having a "problem with authority" or "coloring outside the lines." In contrast, the "employee mind-set" is characterized as "playing it safe." Countless articles and blogs have been written to encourage risk-averse wage-workers to stop "blaming, complaining, and justifying" and instead, "break free of the employee mind-set," "fly with the eagles," and "build wealth," as entrepreneurs do (Wronski 2013). Such expressions reinforce the positive ideology associated with being an entrepreneur, while dismissing the benefits associated with steady employment. However, in my previous research (2013), not all entrepreneurs enthusiastically embrace entrepreneurship. In fact, many minority and women entrepreneurs reported working eighty hours per week (double that of full-time wage work), being unable to take vacations or spend "enough" time with their families, feeling anxiety and stress about making enough money to pay themselves and their workers, and wondering whether their businesses could make it through tough economic times like the recent recession. So although some middle class entrepreneurs report being "happier"—because they have achieved a sense of autonomy, often make more than they did as employees, or left jobs where they were undervalued or exploited—others who continue to struggle for survival are not so sure.

Still another approach to identifying entrepreneurs highlights the role of group membership in fostering business. This body of research focuses on "ethnic entrepreneurship," defined simply as immigrant and ethnic minority business owners. Against the archetype of the "rugged individualist," ethnic entrepreneurs are described as favoring a collectivist approach to business such as relying or depending on their co-ethnic kin and community for resources and support like providing a source of cheap, co-ethnic labor, informal lending, or a targeted customer-base. Through shared ethnic networks and solidarity, immigrant entrepreneurs and their descendants benefit from their co-ethnic community context, which offers a safer and more welcoming avenue of economic integration into the U.S. economy than that of the formal, English-speaking, labor market.

These various definitions are further complicated by the types of occupations in which entrepreneurs may engage. Marginal, low-skilled, and part-time self-employed workers are sometimes called "survival entrepreneurs," like day laborers or domesticas; full-time, mid-range occupations also qualify, such as managers or operators of franchises or family-owned businesses; so too, do high-skilled, technological occupations or those requiring specialized knowledge such as being a doctor or lawyer in private practice or a software engineer who works as an independent or sole contractor.

Finally, entrepreneurs may work in the informal, illicit, or formal economies, although there is some debate as to whether selling one's day labor, oranges, drugs on street corners "count" as entrepreneurship. For example, small-scale vending in rural areas of immigrant settlement is a type of entrepreneurial activity that is often overlooked. However, mobile food vending (e.g. in push carts or "taco trucks") provides an important alternative to formal work, especially among undocumented and unskilled immigrants who face the threat of deportation outside of their immigrant communities, and blocked mobility or exploitive working conditions in the formal labor market. This type of informal enterprise takes place outside of, or coexists alongside, the formal economy. Such "businesses," however, do not always conform to the legal and government regulations and conditions of work associated with those in the formal economy such as paying taxes, complying with health and safety regulations, compensating workers appropriately by applying minimum wage standards, and the like. Additionally, this activity does not generally provide a platform for economic mobility or avenue into the capitalist class, although it may provide a crucial source of income. In a study of mobile food vendors in Texas, my colleagues and I (2012) found that undocumented Mexican immigrant food vendors derived 50 to 100 percent of their income from small-scale vending activities, which included selling fruits and vegetables, popsicles, and "Mexican street corn." The emergence of mobile vending in impoverished immigrant neighborhoods corresponds to the high rates of food insecurity and poor access to grocery stores and supermarkets, areas that are sometimes dubbed "food deserts." The relationship between food access and food vending in areas devoid of traditional grocery stores or markets reveals a resiliency and adaptive creativity among vendors that at least hints at an entrepreneurial spirit, in the classic sense, even though this underground activity is not typically associated with economic progress or growth.

In sum, the definition of what an entrepreneur is remains elusive. An entrepreneur may be innovative and creative, but what these characteristics mean vary as well. An entrepreneur may develop and sell something new, or put existing things together in a new way, or provide a new service. An entrepreneur may be a manager, an operator, or a leader; however, these skills are not limited to entrepreneurs as a variety of occupations held by employees require similar talents. An entrepreneur may be engaged in formal, informal, or illicit enterprises. An entrepreneur is often but not always a risk-taker, and in fact, some of the most successful entrepreneurs redirect risk further down the supply chain to smaller subcontractors or self-employed suppliers. The contradictions and intangibles of the term lead Paul De-Masi (2004) in his brief Defining Entrepreneurship, to conclude somewhat cynically:

> So we are left with a range of factors and behaviors which identify entre-preneurship in some individuals. All of the above tends to reinforce the view that it is difficult, if not impossible to define what an entrepreneur is, and that the word itself can best be used in the past tense to describe a successful business owner.

It is tempting to accept this most basic (non-)definition; however, it is worthwhile to consider that the combination of factors discussed above may better explain what an entrepreneur is. Still left unexplained, then, is what an entrepreneur does.

What Is Entrepreneurship?

Not surprisingly, the definition of entrepreneurship is also imprecise. In a classic work, Peter Kilby (1971; 2003) used a metaphor of an imaginary animal, the Heffalump, to describe entrepreneurship:

It is a large and important animal which has been hunted by many individuals using various ingenious trapping devices. . . . All who claim to have caught sight of him report that he is enormous, but they disagree on his particularities. Not having explored his current habitat with sufficient care, some hunters have used as bait their own favourite dishes and have then tried to persuade people that what they caught was a Heffalump. However, very few are convinced, and the search goes on.

(Kilby 1971: 1)

At its most basic, perhaps, entrepreneurship might be defined simply as starting a new business. Yet, Tom Eisenmann (2013), a professor of business administration at Harvard Business School, offers a more nuanced meaning that may also help with the definition of an entrepreneur. Eisenmann (2013) starts with the definition of **entrepreneurship** offered by his colleague, Howard Stevenson: "entrepreneurship is the pursuit of opportunity beyond resources controlled." Eisenmann under-scores the salience of the words "pursuit" and "opportunity" as capturing the central features of entrepreneurs who seek to develop enterprises:

- "Pursuit" implies a singular, relentless focus . . . entrepreneurs have a sense of urgency that is seldom seen in established companies, where any opportunity is part of a portfolio and resources are more readily available.
- "Opportunity" may entail: 1) pioneering a truly innovative product, 2) devising a new business model, 3) creating a better or cheaper version of an existing product, or 4) targeting an existing product to a new set of customers.
- "Beyond resources controlled" implies resource constraints.

Eisenmann concludes, "Because they are pursuing a novel opportunity while lacking access to required resources, entrepreneurs face considerable risk."

This definition restricts entrepreneurship to the start-up phase; however, it is flexible enough to allow for a variety of organizations and establishments, from mom and pop stores to large corporations. Though this concept of enterprise may encompass a consideration of multiple, contradictory, and sometimes absent chara-cteristics, practices, and motivations that are brought together in different combin-ations to distinguish all entrepreneurs engaged in this activity, ultimately the definition rests on the central and fundamental feature that all entrepreneurs must do to be successful—"manage risk and mobilize resources."

Importantly, this definition also fits the case of the entrepreneur who eventually fails, because the entrepreneurial actor qualifies as an entrepreneur *for as long as he or she is in pursuit of opportunity*. Thus, this concept provides a dynamic and flexible definition of entrepreneurship for the goals of this book, which is to explain a variety of entrepreneurs and their enterprises, including the would-be entrepreneur, the ethnic entrepreneur, the survival entrepreneur, the elite entrepreneur, entrepreneurs of small or large businesses, and entrepreneurs who succeed or fail as well as entrepreneurs with multiple and intersecting identities in favorable or unfavorable structural contexts—in other words, the American entrepreneur.

DISCUSSION QUESTIONS

1. What are some of the competing definitions for "entrepreneur"? What makes it so difficult to reach a consensus on the meaning of this concept?
2. Go online and look for articles and blogs on entrepreneurship. Is there a general message about whether entrepreneurship is good or bad for the entrepreneur, the society, and the economy? What types of entrepreneurs are portrayed? What does the "ideal" entrepreneur look like?
3. Economists, journalists, and the entrepreneurs themselves seem to suggest that entrepreneurship is always a good thing. Why do you think society promotes entrepreneurship in this way? Can you think of some reasons why being an entrepreneur might not always be a positive economic activity?

II: Entrepreneurs Striving for the American Dream

～～～

"I really believe that entrepreneurship is about being able to face failure, manage failure, and succeed after failing."

Kiran Mazumdar-Shaw, founder of Biocon

D o you believe that with hard work and perseverance anyone can achieve the American Dream of owning and operating a successful business? The experience of **ethnic entrepreneurs** or immigrant and ethnic minority business owners would seem to lend credibility to this claim: Korean grocers, Chinese launderers, and Cuban restaurateurs often achieve phenomenal rates of business ownership and economic mobility. A classic theory of immigrant enterprise attributes entrepreneurial success among immigrants and their descendants to essential ethnic group features. For example, strong ethnic networks may generate **social capital** or the access to resources and support based on group membership, which helps members to start a business and keep it going. Social capital resources can be economic or social, such as a source of financial capital, like receiving a loan from an ethnic rotating credit network, or a source of business information such as that provided by an ethnic business association. Yet, a closer look at this body of research reveals that typical ethnic entrepreneurs, such as Korean grocers or Cuban restaurateurs, are disproportionately middle class and male. For example, the first significant wave of Cuban migrants was comprised of a highly educated and elite class, who entered the United States as political refugees in the 1960s.

Cubans fleeing the communist regime in Cuba were largely comprised of a White, professional, and managerial class that settled in a concentrated ethnic enclave in Florida that became known as "Little Havana." This refugee population benefited from a close-knit community and U.S. government support, which included the legal right to live in the United States and, with the passage by Congress of the Cuban Adjustment Act of 1966, granted $1.3 billion for Cuban refugees to learn English, go to school, and start businesses. Perhaps not surprisingly, a thriving Cuban entrepreneurial class and ethnic economy soon followed.

Unlike the Cuban refugee experience, the long history of Mexican migration to the U.S. can be characterized as a revolving door of low-skilled, low-wage, and often undocumented immigrants on the one hand or authorized (legal) but often poor and uneducated "family reunification" migrants on the other. As such, Mexican Americans have been much less likely to engage in entrepreneurship than Cuban Americans. Mexican immigrant women in the United States are particularly disadvantaged. They are much less likely to own a business than their U.S.-born or male counterparts; when they do, they typically make less money than they would if they remained low-wage workers in the low-skilled labor market (Valdez 2011). Diminished outcomes among these survival entrepreneurs suggest an American dream denied—or at least severely dampened. The story of Monica Rivera, a young, undocumented, brown-skinned, Mexican immigrant woman interviewed for my book on Latino/a entrepreneurs (Valdez 2011: 76–77), is illustrative of this more disadvantaged experience.

Monica Rivera: A Mexican American Entrepreneur

In 2009, twenty-two-year-old Monica Rivera and her mother, Theresa, opened a small Mexican restaurant located in a Houston strip mall, flanked by a Domino's Pizza and a dry cleaners. At the time, Monica and her parents were undocumented, having crossed the border illegally from Mexico to the United States in 1991. Unlike her mother and father, who did not complete elementary school and are monolingual Spanish speakers, Monica speaks English and Spanish fluently and earned a high school diploma. After her father had a stroke and was no longer able to work, Monica suggested to her mother that they go into business for themselves. Monica and Theresa had gained valuable experience working in customer service for small retail stores. Like other American entrepreneurs, Monica reasoned that by owning their own business, her family could "rise up in life." She also wanted her mother, who was sometimes mistreated by her employer and customers, to "be her own boss," which would enable her to avoid the sexism, racism, and labor abuses that many employees in the service industry endure.

After a concerted effort to save $10,000 and the difficult decision to sell their property in Mexico for $25,000, they started their own business. The money that they invested in their business covered the cost of the restaurant's lease and some equipment and supplies. Monica's extended family helped with needed repairs, including a new coat of paint on the walls and fixing the floor. Her friends who owned a furniture store gave her a good price on restaurant items. At the time of this interview, *Casa Picante* was sparsely furnished with five tables and chairs, a self-serve soda dispenser, and a home stereo system. In lieu of menus, customers approached a buffet-style counter and simply ordered the items that they could see through a glass partition. A typical morning's options might include rice, beans, eggs, bacon, chicharrón, fresh tortillas, pico de gallo, salsa, and tortilla chips.

With their limited education, lack of experience, and no business plan, Monica and Theresa struggled to break even, let alone make a profit. They made many mistakes that caused them further economic distress. For example, during a particularly slow month, they failed to make a payment on payroll taxes, which resulted in an "embarrassing" visit by IRS agents who demanded payment, levied a fine, and threatened legal action for continued nonpayment. At times, Monica had to borrow money from family members just to keep the lights on and pay household expenses. Monica eventually made the difficult decision to return to minimum-wage work. She explained, "We've had some hard times ... that's why I [got] another job. If [the restaurant makes money] my mother [gets] all the income ... I don't get paid from here." As disadvantaged entrepreneurs living day to day, Monica and Theresa could not afford to keep the business going for too long without turning a profit. They ultimately closed their doors at the nadir of the nationwide economic recession, less than one year after opening (Valdez 2011: 96).

Monica Rivera's story poses a challenge to the American Dream ideology that through hard work and determination, anyone can succeed in business ownership. And she is not alone. According to the National Restaurant Association's conservative estimate, 30 percent of restaurants fail in the first year and 60 percent fail within two years. Factors that lead to business failure include the business owner's lack of experience, insufficient capital to keep the business going, and competition. For Monica and her mother, these factors were compounded by their disadvantaged social location as poor, Mexican immigrant women with limited education. Their story is all too common; yet, it does not reflect fully the American business landscape. There are business owners who achieve the American Dream, and a closer look at those who do may shed some light on the ofen unseen factors that matter for entrepreneurial success rooted in their individual, group, and structural locations.

Sophia Amoruso: The "Self-Made" Entrepreneur

As a teenager, Sophia Amoruso was diagnosed with ADD and depression, hated high school, shoplifted occasionally, and worked at Subway. As a young adult, she dropped out of community college, worked at a few dead-end jobs, and—during a particularly trying low point—moved home to recover from a hernia operation at the age of twenty-two. It was there, while recovering, that she decided to open a vintage clothing store on ebay (Amoroso 2014). Today, at thirty years of age, she is the founder and CEO of the fastest growing retailer in 2011 (Fenn 2013). She has been profiled in Forbes, Entrepreneur, INC, and the Wall Street Journal. Just last year, Entrepreneur Magazine labeled her one of a handful of women entrepreneurs to watch. In 2013, her net income was over $20 million and her Nasty Girl online clothing store reported sales of over $100 million.

In a recent 2014 Slate story, "The Self-Made Man: The Story of An American Myth," John Swansburg notes that Amoruso's autobiography, #GIRLBOSS, presents ". . . a surprisingly traditional self-made narrative." Like Benjamin Franklin, the quintessential self-made man, Swansburg explains that Amoruso "foregrounds her rise by dwelling on her low beginnings," including her parents' unexceptional middle class lifestyle and occasional financial misfortune (which included filing for bankruptcy when Sophia was ten-years-old); moving out as a teenager to live in a series of dilapidated apartments; a job checking student IDs at a San Francisco art school; and a flirtation with dumpster diving and freeganism (Swansburg 2014). At the same time, she underscores her intrinsic entrepreneurial spirit, suggesting in an interview with Forbes that entrepreneurs are born not made. Forbes reports that "entrepreneurial blood courses through her Greek-American family," from her grandfather, the owner of a hotel and music shop, to her mother, a real estate agent. In her autobiography, which is currently being sold on Amazon.com under the subject heading "motivation and self-improvement," she embraces capitalism as meritocratic, stating "it's a kind of alchemy. You combine hard work, creativity, and self-determination, and things start to happen" (2014: 16). She also emphasizes an ideology of rugged individualism, writing, "a #GIRLBOSS is someone who's in charge of her own life. She gets what she wants because she works for it . . . [she] take[s] control and accept[s] responsibility . . . (2014: 10)." In the end, she bemoans the business and corporate media's portrayal of her as "a savvy ingénue with a rags-to-riches story," although it is clear that she does not reject it outright either (2014: 11).

How can we explain the different trajectories of business success and failure experienced by Monica and Sophia? Both women were twenty-two-year-olds when they went into business, and neither had much money or education to start with. Each determined that by being her "own boss," she would be better off. They also had in common some of the traits that are often ascribed to entrepreneurs, including risk-taking behavior, channeling a positive attitude, and a belief in individual responsibility and self-reliance. And although they have experienced wildly different outcomes, both can be described as **necessity entrepreneurs**. A necessity entrepreneur engages in business ownership because of economic uncertainty or unemployment—in Monica's case her father's inability to work compromised her family's household income and prompted her business aspirations; in Sophia's case, her own health, financial concerns, and unemployment compelled her to start a small business out of her mother's home. Nevertheless, Monica Rivera returned to low-wage work within the first (and last) year of her restaurant, whereas Sophia Amoruso, in less than ten years, has achieved remarkable success and is by all accounts living the American Dream.

Early studies of eighteenth and nineteenth century American entrepreneurship tended to ascribe certain values and attitudes to successful entrepreneurs only, which included being hard working, thrifty, honest, ambitious, self-reliant, optimistic, risk-taking, creative, innovative, and responsible. Other studies focused on developing a demographic profile of the North American business elite. These analyses revealed that economically successful business owners were more likely to be U.S.-born, European American, male, living and working in an urban area, possessing above average **human capital** (i.e., education and work experience), and growing up in a middle or upper class household. These characteristics remain salient for contemporary entrepreneurial success. For example, Zissimopoulos and Karoly (2007) examined the relationship between health, wealth, and entrepreneurship. They found that older, healthier, and wealthier men were more likely to become entrepreneurs because they had accumulated the necessary work experience and financial capital, often from personal savings, to do so. In their study of American entrepreneurs, Fairlie and Robb (2008) observed that white men reported higher rates of business ownership than blacks, Latinos, or Asians; however, they also noted that foreign-born ethnic groups often surpassed their U.S.-born counterparts in entrepreneurial participation. Finally, possessing **entrepreneurial capital**, or a familiarity with business ownership that is often linked to a father's experience, increases the likelihood of being an entrepreneur. In a study of almost 200 entrepreneurs born around the nineteenth century (1800–1899), more than half reported that their father owned a business (Sarachek 1978: 449), a trend that continues to this day (Fairlie and Robb 2007). These historical and contemporary studies show that there is little support for the Horatio Alger's "rags to riches" narrative. The majority of successful entrepreneurs grew up in middle or upper class households or were children of the business elite. In fact, prior research suggests that less than 15 percent of the American business elite can be traced back to working or lower class origins (Sarachek 1978: 451).

There are marked differences between Sophia Amoruso and the successful business owners described above—especially as they relate to gender and education—yet, she shares with them many other characteristics, including her racial classification as white, her family's middle-class privilege, her entrepreneurial capital (grandfather and mother), her urban geography, and her values and attitudes. The traditional portrait of the successful, white, middle class entrepreneur, then, seems to fit Sophia well. Nevertheless, she also stands apart from this group in significant ways. In particular, as a woman without a college degree, she did not have access to the social and business networks that foster enterprise among white male elites, what is sometimes referred to as the Old Boys' Club. This informal social network serves to keep money, power, and wealth in the hands of elite, white businessmen. The resources and support Sophia enjoyed were more modest. For example, her ability to move home and live rent-free with all expenses paid while she established her fledgling business was central to her success. She also enjoyed social capital resources stemming from her middle class status, which included owning a personal computer, having access to the internet at home, and possessing the skills needed to learn, navigate, and construct an online presence, from developing her online shop to capitalizing on social media to promote sales (Amoroso 2014). The timing of her business was also critical. She started her online business in California at a time when the dot-com era was recovering and expanding. In much the same way that the invention of the sewing machine and demand for ready to wear clothing during the industrial revolution opened up opportunities for Jewish immigrant tailors in New York to start businesses, the emerging online marketplace created the possibility and opportunity for Sophia's business idea to first crystallize and then to flourish.

Although Monica could be similarly characterized as hard working, responsible, positive, and desiring of autonomy for herself and her mother, the similarities between Monica and Sophia—and white middle class entrepreneurs more generally—ended there. As a poor, uneducated, undocumented, young woman of color with few social support networks and even fewer economic resources, Monica's entrepreneurial spirit was not sufficient to overcome her disadvantaged social and economic position. And while starting a business during an economic downturn is characteristic of necessity entrepreneurs, the economic uncertainty she and her family experienced also affected more established businesses and hit her community hard, which decreased her customer base and her profit. While other business owners borrowed money or extended credit lines to keep afloat, Monica had no such recourse.

Notably, there is a large and growing population of poor, undocumented, Mexican (and Central American) immigrant women who are turning to business ownership in the United States. Specifically, they work on their own account as self-employed domesticas, such as house cleaners, maids, and nannies (Hondagneu-Sotelo 2001). This type of work is generally portrayed as an informal economic activity because it is unstable, insecure, and is "off the books," meaning there is little to no government oversight and women are generally paid under the table. So although Mexican immigrant women like Monica are unlikely to become wildly successful business tycoons, many are engaged in necessity entrepreneurship. For these disadvantaged women, their unorthodox self-employment activity is, first and foremost, a strategy of survival (Valenzuela 2001: 349).

In comparing Sophia Amoruso's story with Monica Rivera's, it is clear that merely the attitudes and values that business owners express are inadequate to ensure entrepreneurial success. Likewise, the conventional approach to understanding entrepreneurship has focused on "rugged individualists" who achieve success through determination and innovation, or "ethnic entrepreneurs" who rely on ethnic ties and collectivist ideologies to gain a foothold in business. Yet these narratives fail to consider fully the hidden contributions of collective social and economic resources available to these middle class and male elite businessmen and that largely undergird their success.

Sociologists concerned with **social stratification**, or the unequal distribution of power, wealth, and status, suggest that the American society is comprised of intersecting systems of inequality based on race, class, and gender, as well as other categories of identity, such as disability, legal status, and the like. Feminist scholars of color have contended that, to fully understand stratification in the United States, we must consider how these and other intersectional identities combine in a "matrix of domination" or the ways in which these identities are hierarchically organized within the American social structure (Collins 1990: 18). As Patricia Hill Collins wrote in her groundbreaking work, *Black Feminist Thought: Knowledge, Consciousness, and the Politics of Empowerment*:

> The significance of seeing race, class, and gender as interlocking systems of oppression is that such an approach fosters a paradigmatic shift of thinking inclusively about other oppressions, such as age, sexual orientation, religion, and ethnicity. Race, class, and gender represent the three systems of oppression that most heavily affect African-American women. But these systems and the economic, political, and ideological conditions that support them may not be the most fundamental oppressions, and they certainly affect many more groups than Black women. Other people of color, Jews, the poor white women, and gays and lesbians have all had similar ideological justifications offered for their subordination.
>
> (Collins 1990: 222–223)

In the United States, entrepreneurs are unequally positioned within the social structure based on their multiple and intersectional identities. These factors, more than personal values, shape their entrepreneurial success. From an intersectional perspective, Sophia enjoyed certain privileges associated with her racial and class positions; however, as a woman, she was positioned at the bottom of the gender hierarchy. Her distinct yet intersecting positions of privilege and oppression combined to explain the hardships she experienced early in her life, but that, ultimately, conditioned the resources she needed to succeed in business. In contrast and as a poor and undocumented woman of color, Monica faced multiple oppressions based on her intersectional position at the bottom of gender, class, and even legal status hierarchies; in the end, she was unable to overcome the disadvantages associated with her social location. Taken together, the entrepreneurial experiences of Sophia and Monica demonstrate how larger structural forces can restrict and work against the entrepreneurial success of hardworking women and facilitate the reproduction of social and economic inequality. In other words, intersecting forms of racial, gender, and class stratification are a product of structural forces beyond the control of individuals. The ability of an individual woman to access the various forms of capital needed to launch and sustain a business are mediated by her ethnic, racial, and class positions, as well as gender hierarchies. Access to different forms of capital is unevenly distributed along racial, ethnic, class, and gender lines with middle class or elite European (white) American men more likely to have greater access to the forms of capital that are needed to launch and sustain a business. Ultimately, by applying an intersectional approach to American enterprise situated within the larger economy and society, multiple and intersecting forms of inequality are uncovered to better explain the forces that condition success. An intersectional approach to entrepreneurship sets the stage for a serious reconsideration of the promise and pitfalls of business ownership and the relationship between American entrepreneurship and the American Dream.

DISCUSSION QUESTIONS

1. The stories of Monica Rivera and Sophia Amoruso depict wildly divergent economic outcomes; yet, both Monica and Sophia are both women who were raised in working-class homes. What are some of the individual, group, and structural factors that help explain their different trajectories of success?
2. The American Creed ideology suggests that with hard work, drive, and ambition, anyone can achieve the American Dream of owning a successful business. This ideology is rooted in the idea that the United States is a "meritocracy," or the notion that power and rewards are distributed to Americans based on their abilities and skills. How does the concept of social stratification complicate or challenge this deeply held belief?
3. In the United States, the American Dream means different things to different people. It could mean owning a business, a home, or for parents, a better life for the next generation. What is your idea of the American Dream? Is the American Dream always tied to economic or financial gain?

III: Are American Entrepreneurs as Diverse as We Think?

Understanding Trends and Group Differences

꩜

A t 13 percent of the working age population, the United States of America boasts the highest rate of entrepreneurship among twenty-five industrialized economies. Economist Robert Fairlie, who analyzes data on entrepreneurship for the Kauffman Foundation, noted that in *each month* of 2013, the U.S. economy added 476,000 new business owners. These numbers are consistent with most Americans' strongly held belief that the United States is the land of opportunity, where with hard work and a good idea, anyone can own a business. A higher percentage of Americans hold this belief than in any other nation. In a 2013 report published by the Global Entrepreneurship Monitor (2014), fully 47 percent of Americans agreed that good opportunities for new businesses exist, and 56 percent "believed they had the capabilities to launch a business."

In addition to a strong belief in the American Dream, entrepreneurs share some key characteristics and attitudes that motivate them to engage in business ownership. Chief among them are the desires to be their "own boss" and to "make money" or at least more money than they did as wage workers or in the face of unemployment. Georgellis and colleagues (2007) concluded that these two key determinants predicted not only entry into business ownership, but also whether business owners stayed in business over the long term. Other characteristics ubiquitous among business owners include a strong work ethic, a positive outlook, and a tendency toward risk.

Moreover, American entrepreneurs are a diverse group. The U.S. is first among twenty-five industrialized countries in the number of women engaged in enterprise; one out of every ten businesses is owned by a woman. Immigrants also make up a significant portion of American entrepreneurs. The Small Business Administration reports that 10.5 percent of immigrants own a business in the U.S., compared to

9 percent of their native-born counterparts. Most immigrant-owned businesses are small family-owned restaurants or "mom and pop" shops; however, a significant portion of these businesses are elite firms and large corporations. In fact, 40 percent of today's Fortune 500 companies were founded by immigrants or their descendants. Racial minorities are also engaged in business ownership. Fully 35 percent of business owners are people of color, including Latinos, who own 10 percent of all businesses. Finally, with age comes wisdom, including the experience, confidence, and ability to start a business, as observed in the uptick in business ownership over the life course, with 16 percent of business owners under thirty-five years of age, 33 percent between the ages of thirty-five and forty-nine, and over half (51 percent) over the age of fifty.

American entrepreneurs are a sizeable and diverse population, lending credence to the belief that people from all walks of life can succeed in starting their own business. Yet this belief is also challenged by findings from research that takes an intersectional approach. This research investigates disparities in business ownership across race, class, and gender. Social stratification, which is defined as the unequal positioning of groups within the larger economy and society, has an effect on entrepreneurial outcomes. After all, differences in resources and other inequalities affect group members' ability to start, maintain, and grow a business. In other words, imbalances at the starting line of business ownership often persist at the finish line, leading to varying rates of success. It is essential to understand and identify the factors that help explain why some groups succeed and others fail. An intersectional and comparative approach to research on groups within the stratified American society allows us to better understand how systems of oppression and privilege condition the entrepreneurial fortunes of distinct groups.

Entrepreneurial outcomes differ along the lines of race, class, and gender. That is because these common social divisions condition differences at the individual, group, and structural levels. At the individual level, **human capital**, or education and work experience, is associated with increased entrepreneurial participation: higher-skilled workers are more likely to enter business ownership than their lower-skilled counterparts. At the group level, **social capital** resources, such as family members who can provide unpaid labor or co-ethnic community groups that lend money, facilitate entrepreneurship among members of particular groups. Finally, at the structural level, the "**context of reception**," or the economic and social climate that favors or disfavors a new business, can differ for entrepreneurs of different races, classes, or genders.

Specifically, the context of reception includes government policies, such as subsidized business loans for women, minorities, or refugees, and the opportunity structure of the economy, such as the need for certain industries, goods, or services. For example, the presence of a strong ethnic enclave may help co-ethnic members gain a foothold in business, whereas a climate of heightened nativism or racism may make business ownership more difficult for immigrants or racial minorities. In a highly stratified economy and society, these individual, group, and structural-level factors combine to create differences in participation across groups. Accordingly, business success is in many ways influenced by the entrepreneur's individual and collective identity within a particular context.

Women Entrepreneurs

The U.S. Census reports that the proportion of women who own businesses in the United States is on the rise. In 2012, approximately one out of ten women owned a business, accounting for 36 percent of business owners, or 7.8 million firms. Elite women entrepreneurs, who own firms with revenues of $1 million or more, increased their ranks by over 50 percent in the last decade. In an executive report published by The Global Entrepreneurship and Development Institute, researchers concluded that the United States was ranked number one of thirty countries that provided favorable conditions for women's entrepreneurship. These numbers suggest that today, women enjoy greater opportunities to engage in business ownership than ever before, with America leading the way.

Yet these positive developments only tell part of the story. Women-owned businesses have not reached parity with male-owned businesses. Firms owned by women underperform firms owned by men across a variety of measures, including business longevity, sales, and number of employees (Robb 2002). The 2007 Survey of Business Owners found that, when comparing a portion of firms that are owned by sole proprietors only, women-owned firms generated a total of $1.2 trillion in receipts and accounted for 6.4 percent of total employment, while men-owned firms generated $8.5 trillion in receipts and accounted for 35 percent of total employment. While women's ownership share of elite firms has grown, only 2 percent of women-owned firms report revenue of $1 million or more, and of that 2 percent, only a small fraction (15 percent) report revenue of $10 million or more. At best, women reach only 60 percent of men's success in enterprise (Fairlie and Robb 2009).

Some researchers explain these gender disparities as related to differences between men and women in their reasons for starting a business. For example, some researchers argue that achieving a work-life balance may be more important for women than men; women may make decisions regarding their businesses that result in less positive economic outcomes. Likewise, research shows that women entrepreneurs often express success in terms of non-pecuniary criteria such as personal growth, interpersonal relations, and a concern for others (Valdez 2011). These explanations suggest that there may be some truth to the claim that women and men engage in business ownership for different reasons; however, there is little evidence to suggest that women entrepreneurs are less interested in being independent or making money than men or that differences in motivations explain the gender gap in entrepreneurship.

Among women business owners, there are differences in entrepreneurial participation and success along racial and ethnic lines. In particular, Latinas represent one of the fastest growing entrepreneurial segments in the country, in line with increases in the entrepreneurial participation of Latino/as of any gender. In the last five years, Latina business ownership increased by almost 50 percent. This rate of growth is much higher than the 20 percent increase observed for women-owned businesses as a whole during this same period. Today, approximately one out of every ten women-owned businesses is owned by a Latina. Last year, the revenue generated by Latina business owners totaled $66 billion.

In my qualitative study with Latino/a entrepreneurs I found that, like most entrepreneurs, they expressed a desire to be independent and successful (Valdez 2011: 99). However, they did not always define success in terms of economic progress. For Latinas, success was sometimes associated with non-economic factors, such as restaurateurs' joy of cooking, the opportunity to share the goods they created or the food they made, the loyalty of their staff ("I treat them like family"), or having a "regular" customer base. For example, Rita, a forty-seven-year-old Mexican-origin naturalized citizen, opened a Mexican food restaurant as a "challenge" to herself. After two years in business, her restaurant was just "breaking even," which means that the business was generating enough revenue to stay open but was not making a profit. Still, she claimed that she was a successful business owner because she "made her own hours" and her customers were happy. Similarly, Maria, a forty-four-year-old Mexican immigrant woman, argued that she was successful because "success comes from how you treat your clients, your enthusiasm. . . . When people finish eating and you ask them how the meal was and they tell you it was great."

These expressions of non-economic success seem to reinforce gender stereotypes; that in the process of gender socialization, women entrepreneurs are oriented toward different goals than men such that women seek to achieve non-pecuniary markers of success. Yet the interviews also revealed a desire for independence and to make money, even as some women fell short of these goals. Most Latina entrepreneurs expressed disappointment when their businesses failed to make a profit. For example, Maria reasoned that because she quit school after second grade, she did not have the skills to be "more [economically] successful." Rita believed that she would have made a better income if she had worked for someone else, though she affirmed that her success was based on more than money. The Latina entrepreneurs who participated in my research thus defined success in shifting terms; they were more likely to express non-economic indicators of success in the face of economic stagnation. These findings underscore the need for research that examines the intersections of race and gender in American enterprise.

Mounting evidence suggests that women entrepreneurs lag behind men because of structural forces rather than individual motivations or personal decisions. The United States is a patriarchal society, organized hierarchically by gender. In a patriarchal system, men are ascribed the primary authority and responsibility over family and community. Patriarchy justifies the maintenance and reproduction of men's power and control over women's labor in the public and domestic spheres, as observed in the "persistent fact" of gender stratification and discrimination in occupations, promotions, and wage inequality in the American labor market (Browne and Misra 2003) and the devaluation of household work and women's access to family and household resources, like unpaid family labor or inheritance, when compared to men (Browne and Misra 2003).

For example, in my research with middle class entrepreneurs (Valdez 2015), I found that disparities in inheritance in the form of wealth, assets, or the family business itself are conditioned by gender: inheritance was almost always reserved for the sons of middle class entrepreneurs. The experience of Cecilia M., the owner of a successful temporary worker and executive recruiting and consulting firm in El Paso, offers some insight into the relationship between gender and inheritance. Cecilia M. grew up in an upper middle class household with a successful entrepreneurial father, a stay-at-home mother, and nine siblings. She credits her father's business acumen with sparking her own interest in business.

> You know, I think that when you grow up in a family that has their own business, it definitely can be an influence on you as to what you choose to do because you're around it, and you see it, and you kind of live it . . . instead of going back to teaching [after my divorce], I really, really liked the business world . . .

Cecilia's family history of business ownership, or **entrepreneurial capital**, shaped her own desire to start a business. Yet the gendered realities of Cecilia's middle class family and household limited her ability to translate that entrepreneurial capital into owning her own business initially.

Cecilia's middle class parents expected all ten of their children to pursue a college education—a marker of middle class culture—regardless of gender. Yet they encouraged their daughters to pursue traditional gendered occupations only, specifically in nursing or teaching. Their sons, on the other hand, were advised to earn business degrees in preparation to take over one of their father's multiple businesses in due time. Cecilia and her sisters were also expected to marry and have children, which her parents felt should take priority over college or work. Cecilia followed her parent's wishes and pursued a teaching career. She worked as a teacher until she married, when she took her parent's advice again, and quit teaching to focus on being a housewife and mother. Unfortunately, her marriage did not work out and she and her husband eventually filed for divorce. She needed money so she asked her father for help. He gave her a job working as a secretary in one of his businesses. Shortly thereafter, she decided to embark on a business of her own.

Cecilia's transition from divorced mother to business owner reveals how parents' gendered attitudes affect their children's entrepreneurial pursuits. When she finally decided to go into business for herself, she approached her father for financial support, which he provided. His generosity to his daughter, however, paled in comparison to that which he conferred upon his sons, especially with regard to inheritance. With each graduation, a son received one of his father's businesses outright. Unlike the sons, Cecilia and her sisters were not given the opportunity to take over one of their father's multiple businesses. Instead, Cecilia developed and brought the initial idea for her business venture to her dad and after convincing him it was viable he agreed to lend financial support. As a condition of his financial support, however, her father demanded that the business and its profits be distributed equally among her four sisters, three of whom were salaried-workers and one who was a stay-at-home-mom. Cecilia's story confirms the findings of previous studies, which demonstrate that men tend to acquire more wealth and property through inheritance than women (Conley and Ryvicker 2005; Warren et al. 2001). Her story also demonstrates how gender affects the unequal distribution of wealth and assets within the same family and household. Gender disparities in the distribution of wealth and inheritance within a family set the stage for unequal opportunities in enterprise.

Women entrepreneurs are often the primary caretakers of their families. As a consequence, they may work fewer hours than men, prioritize a more flexible schedule or a "work-life" balance, and even forgo expanding a successful business. Gender disparities are also associated with women's lower human capital attainment (education and work experience), limited access to financial capital and economic resources (personal savings, access to credit), fewer social or business networks that provide economic resources and social support, and constraints on women's entrance into industries and occupations traditionally dominated by men (i.e., men own businesses in professional industries and construction; women own businesses in retail and the service sector). These structural factors explain a larger part of men's economic advantage over women entrepreneurs.

Racial Minorities

A recent U.S. Census report indicated that minority-owned businesses increased at twice the national rate of all U.S. businesses between 2002 and 2007. Minority-owned businesses accounted for 20 percent of total businesses during this period, or 5.8 million. The rate of increase and total number of firms varied across minority groups. Black-owned businesses increased by 60 percent to 1.9 million, whereas Latino-owned businesses increased at a slower rate (44 percent), but reported a greater number of businesses overall (2.3 million). Black-owned businesses generated receipts totaling $137 billion while Latino-owned businesses accounted for $345 billion in receipts, or two and a half times that of black-owned businesses (see Table 3.1).

The vast majority (85 percent) of minority entrepreneurs are "self-employed," defined as those who work on their own account with no paid employees. Most of the minority self-employed are concentrated in the low-wage, low-skilled service industries, including repair and maintenance and personal services. Whereas Asians, like non-Hispanic whites, make up a larger share of business owners than their proportion of the total U.S. population (6 percent compared to 5 percent), most racial minorities are underrepresented as business owners proportional to their share of the population (Table 3.1).

Asian Americans

Asian Americans are the most entrepreneurial racial minority group in the United States. This group includes Asian Indian, Chinese, Filipino, Japanese, Korean, Vietnamese, and other Asian ethnic groups. In addition to exceeding their proportion of the U.S. population, Asian-owned businesses also generate higher receipts and employ more people than other racial minorities, including blacks, Latinos, and Native Americans. Of Asian-owned businesses, Chinese account for 27 percent, followed by Asian Indians (20 percent), Vietnamese (15 percent), Koreans (12 percent), and 10 percent each of Filipinos and other Asians.

Scholars of ethnic entrepreneurship suggest that the high rate of Asian American entrepreneurship is attributable to a delayed pattern of assimilation associated with

Table 3.1 Number of U.S. Businesses and Total Receipts by Race, 2007

	% of Total Businesses	% of U.S. Pop (2013)	# of Businesses (millions)	Receipts (billions)
Non-Hispanic White	83.3	62.6	22.6	10300
Black	7.0	13.2	1.9	137
Latino	8.5	17.1	2.3	345
Asian	5.9	5.3	1.6	514
Native American	0.008	1.2	0.02	35
All	100.0	100.0	27.1	30200

ethnic solidarity. This perspective suggests that as Asian immigrants settle in the United States, they rely on their strong ethnic communities for help integrating into the host society. Ethnic solidarity is typified by close-knit, co-ethnic ties that generate reciprocity and enforceable trust. Trust among co-ethnics may provide economic and social resources, such as co-ethnic business networks, a source of low-wage or unpaid labor, and an informal or semi-formal source of financial lending. Ivan Light, a sociologist and expert on Asian entrepreneurship, contends that ethnic-group membership provides a basis for mutual aid (Light 1972). For example, Japanese and Korean rotating credit associations serve as co-ethnic lending institutions that foster capital accumulation. Furthermore, researchers observe that ethnic networks and extended family ties are characteristic of the cultural traditions of Asian immigrants originating from places such as China, Korea, and Japan. Members of ethnic networks facilitate the economic incorporation of other migrants, often through business ownership. Ethnic solidarity also helps Asians to combat a negative context of reception in U.S. mainstream society, where they may face racial discrimination.

The ethnic entrepreneurship paradigm generally maintains that ethnic-based social capital provides an important resource for Asian American entrepreneurs. However, studies that consider individual and structural factors conclude that social capital alone is not sufficient to explain the high rate of Asian American business ownership. The "first wave" of Asian immigrant entrepreneurs in the United States shared additional characteristics that encouraged business ownership. Many belonged to middle or upper-class families and possessed high human capital, including professional or managerial experience in their country of origin. The success of *Kim Son*, a famous Vietnamese-owned family restaurant in Houston, illustrates how human capital, middle-class group membership, and the context of reception all combined to support this family's entrepreneurial success. *Kim Son* was started by the *La* family, a family of nine members who together fled the communist regime in Vietnam to arrive in Houston as refugees in the 1980s. They started one small restaurant located in an ethnic enclave in downtown Houston. Today, their business spans several locations, including a 35,000 square-foot restaurant in Houston's Chinatown. That restaurant was built at a cost of $2 million, and includes such luxuries as marble floors, fresh flowers, and wrought-iron banisters.

Though the *La* family certainly relied on social capital in the form of close-knit family and ethnic ties, they also benefited from their human capital, class position, and structural opportunity in the larger economy. In Vietnam, the family was middle class and had previously owned a successful restaurant. In the United States, they began their business at a time of rising demand for ethnic specialty goods and services and in a favorable context of reception in the form of both government policies that aimed at supporting refugee integration and Houston's established

Vietnamese enclave. Like many Asian-origin entrepreneurs in the United States, the *La* family had access to human and social capital combined with a favorable reception context, which facilitated their entrepreneurial participation and success (Earvolino 1985; Sharpe 1997).

Latino Americans

Recent census figures indicate that Latinos now constitute the largest American minority group. The growth of this population coincided with unprecedented growth in Latino business. The Latino share of American entrepreneurs grew from 10.5 percent in 1996 to almost 20 percent in 2012. Between 2004 and 2014, the number of Latino-owned businesses doubled from 1.5 million to over 3 million. This rate of growth in business ownership was twice that of the general population. This year, the projected combined annual revenue of these businesses is over $450 billion—over $100 billion more than the annual revenue produced by Latino-owned businesses in 2009. The data clearly show that Latino enterprise makes an important contribution to the broader American economy as well as to the Latino community.

Qualitative research shows that Latino entrepreneurs often "give back" to their communities by providing financial and material resources and support to co-ethnics, though the decision to give back may be related to social class. In their qualitative study of 1.5 and second generation Mexicans in Southern California, Jody Agius Vallejo and Jennifer Lee (2009) found that Mexican-origin respondents who were poor as children but transitioned to the middle class as adults were more likely to express a collectivist ideology in their patterns of giving back to poor kin, co-ethnics, and the ethnic community at large. By contrast, Latino respondents who grew up in middle-class households expressed an individualistic ideology consistent with that of non-Hispanic whites; they were less inclined to give back. My research also supports the notion that Latino entrepreneurs help out members of their community, though I found instances of giving back among Latino entrepreneurs regardless of their class position. For example, in my research on Latino restaurant owners in Houston, I met a Mexican American man who provided a scholarship for the purchase of books to one college student each year in the poor Mexican community where he grew up. Likewise, oral histories with elite Mexican American entrepreneurs in El Paso revealed that members sought opportunities to give back. In one instance, a business owner with no children of his own acted as an "angel investor" in his community. He befriended a young Mexican male employee at his favorite local ice cream parlor and offered to pay for that young man's college education. He did so in the hope that the young man would one day take over his prosthetics and orthotics business. The young man worked for the angel investor for some time before opening up his own prosthetics business. Latino entrepreneurs also give back to their communities in less personal ways, by providing ethnic-specific services and hard-to-find specialty items, offering employment to job-seekers who are not yet English proficient and training co-ethnic employees to go into business for themselves.

Latino entrepreneurs also contribute to their families' social and economic progress. Recent estimates show that over 50 percent of Latino business owners report earning over $50,000 in household income, on par with the median household income in the United States; only 35 percent of Latino wage workers report this same household income. Latino business owners are also 85 percent more likely to earn between $100,000 and $150,000 and 300 percent more likely to earn over $150,000 in household income than the Latino population as a whole.

Yet despite these broad indicators, Latino entrepreneurs are a heterogeneous group, and different Latino ethnic groups experience different outcomes in relation to entrepreneurship. For example, Cuban Americans report much higher rates of business ownership than Mexican Americans do; this is due in part to different pre-migration characteristics, including human capital, patterns of migration and settlement (which are related to access to social capital), and contexts of reception, including government policies and the prevalence of social discrimination.

Like Vietnamese immigrants, the first significant wave of Cuban migrants to the U.S. entered the country as political refugees. As such, they benefitted from U.S. government policies providing aid to refugees, including the 1966 Cuban Adjustment Act. This act granted $1.3 billion in financial aid to Cuban refugees, including low-interest college and business loans. The Post-Castro Cuban migration largely comprised members of the professional and managerial classes who settled in a concentrated ethnic enclave in Florida known as "Little Havana"; not surprisingly, a thriving Cuban entrepreneurial class and ethnic economy soon followed.

By contrast, the long history of Mexican migration to the U.S. can be characterized as a revolving door of low-skilled, low-wage, and often unauthorized or temporary labor on the one hand, and authorized family reunification migrants on the other. As such, Mexican Americans are less likely to engage in entrepreneurship than Cuban Americans, and when they do, are less likely to achieve economic mobility or business longevity.

African-Americans

Most studies of ethnic entrepreneurship focus on those groups that disproportionately engage in this activity. These studies also tend to base their explanations for differences in entrepreneurial activity across groups on factors related to ethnicity.

For example, scholars of ethnic entrepreneurship have written extensively on the entrepreneurial success of Koreans and Chinese in the U.S. and on upwardly mobile Cuban business owners. These entrepreneurial groups are understood to share group-based factors that facilitate enterprise, including cohesive communities with collectivist orientations that rely on ethnic solidarity and social capital. In contrast, groups with disproportionately low rates of entrepreneurship, such as African Americans, are often overlooked or dismissed as accidental entrepreneurs who become self-employed as a "survival strategy" and an alternative to unemployment.

Scholars of ethnic entrepreneurship attribute African Americans' negligible rates of enterprise to a number of factors, including limited human capital and a non-cohesive community. This perspective implicates the black community in hindering enterprise and reproducing social and economic disadvantages through ". . . a kind of collective expectation that new arrivals should not be 'uppity' and should not try to surpass, at least at the start, the collective status of their elders" (Portes and Rumbaut 2006: 87). This negative community context reduces opportunities for enterprise. The ethnicity entrepreneurship paradigm concedes that African Americans may face a "negative societal reception," or racism based on "non-phenotypically white" features, which may "hamper mainstream integration" (Pores and Rumbaut 2006).

I conducted research that compared black entrepreneurs with Asians and Latinos. Although my studies (2008; 2011) confirm that black entrepreneurs are less likely to own businesses than Asians or Latinos, my research also showed that black entrepreneurs, like Asian entrepreneurs, relied on their community for co-ethnic support, and like Latinos, sought out opportunities to "give back" to their community. This research revealed that black entrepreneurs' reasons for going into business were similar to those of Asians and Latinos—they craved autonomy and to improve their economic circumstances. Unlike Asians and Latinos groups, however, black entrepreneurs were hindered by their class background, which decreased the quality and quantity of their social capital resources. Renee Tate, a forty-two-year-old black entrepreneur, exemplifies why and how a lack of class and social capital resources hinder business start-up and maintenance among black entrepreneurs (Valdez 2011: 89). She admitted that when she started her business, she did not have the collateral needed to secure a business loan from a bank, and did not possess the skills needed to complete a government-subsidized small business loan for minorities and women. Consequently, she started her business with $35,000 in personal savings alone. When asked whether she turned to any family or friends for additional financial aid before starting her business she replied, somewhat wryly, "normally *I* give money to *them!*" Because she started her business with less than she needed but with all that she had, she quickly fell behind on her lease. To keep the business open, she borrowed an additional $10,000 from her husband's 401K (for which he received a significant penalty for early withdrawal). Renee's disadvantageous start to business ownership was common among black entrepreneurs in my study.

Additionally, black entrepreneurs reported incidents of racial discrimination from suppliers, customers, and others. Unlike other racial and ethnic minorities, however, black entrepreneurs signaled that this unequal treatment was not an individual-level concern, but was rooted in larger structural forces, such as **statistical discrimination** or **institutional racism**, which captures discrimination that takes place within the larger social context, disadvantages that are associated with "the prevailing system of opportunities and constraints favors the success of one group over another … through the ordinary functioning of [society's] cultural, economic, and political systems" (Pager and Shepherd 2008: 17). Their conclusion is supported by research on bank lending showing that minority-owned firms were "denied credit at a higher rate," were "more likely to pay higher interest rates," and experienced "credit discrepancies" more frequently than non-minority firms (Johnson et al. 2002: 19–20). Though disparities between non-minority and minority firms are often attributed to differences in education, work experience, and credit worthiness, there is overwhelming evidence that racial inequality in lending persists "even after controlling for differences in credit worthiness and other factors" (Robb and Fairlie 2006: 26).

Social scientists concerned with economic inequality demonstrate that acquiring wealth, such as a business or property, does not rest simply on individual characteristics like educational attainment or class background. Racial inequalities in wealth creation and its reproduction are rooted in an American social structure that is organized hierarchically along racial and ethnic lines. For example, throughout U.S. history, policies enforced racial segregation and destabilized black communities and other communities of color, producing a legacy of institutional racism and statistical discrimination. Over time, these factors "cemented minority groups to the bottom of society's economic hierarchy" (Oliver and Shapiro 1996: 5). Racism against the black community harmed their entrepreneurial activity to a profound degree at every stage of business development. Because the United States is historically a patriarchal society, gender also shapes wealth acquisition. In the United States, men acquire more property through inheritance than women (Conley and Ryvicker 2005; Warren et al. 2001). Taken together, racial, ethnic, and gender inequalities produce a context wherein white middle-class men inherit wealth at a higher rate than white women or blacks and Latino/as of any gender. In addition, white middle-class men are far more likely to possess entrepreneurial capital—experience in a family-owned business growing up—than white women, Latino/as or blacks.

Non-Hispanic white business owners outperform non-white business owners on a number of measures. First, whites dominate business ownership in the United States. Constituting only 60 percent of the total U.S. population, whites own 80 percent of American businesses. Only one racial minority group, Asians, is overrepresented in business; however, Asian business owners exceed their proportion in the total population by only one percentage point (6 percent versus 5 percent). Second, white business owners report higher sales and receipts than their non-white counterparts. Their receipts, which totaled over $10 trillion in 2007, far exceeded those of racial minorities, whose combined receipts totaled $1 billion, a marked difference. Third, whites' high returns are due in part to their concentration in lucrative and durable industries, including professional, scientific, and technical services and construction, whereas racial minorities are concentrated in non-durable industries and the retail and service sector. Because of their dominance in business ownership, it is not surprising that whites reported a slower rate of growth than racial minorities in the last decade.

The white racial advantage in business ownership is maintained across the intersecting categories of class, gender, and age. For example, white men are more likely to own a business than black, Latino, or Asian men, whereas white women entrepreneurs generally earn more than black, Latino, or Asian women. Moreover, a greater number of elite firms are owned by white men and women; within this prosperous subgroup, white elites generate greater receipts and sales than their immigrant, ethnic, or racial minority counterparts. Yet within the white racial category, class, gender, and age, all mediate success. By examining multiple identities together, we can better understand the influence of race, class, and gender on privilege and oppression. These intersecting dimensions of identity affect entrepreneurship both across and within particular groups, even among whites, who are positioned at the top of the American racial hierarchy.

The White Racial Advantage

In a 2013 study, economists Ross Levine and Yona Rubinstein found that middle class white men were more likely than members of other groups to become successful entrepreneurs in keeping with previous literature. Certainly, their racial, gender, and class background facilitated this group's participation and success. These successful entrepreneurs tended to grow up in wealthier, better-educated households. Before starting their businesses, many successful entrepreneurs were successful wage and salary workers, so the transition from worker to owner only increased their already fortunate economic circumstances. Remarkably, however, the researchers also uncovered the importance of "illicit" tendencies. In particular, they found that successful white, middle class, educated male entrepreneurs scored higher on measures of teenage delinquency than their peers. In their youth, they were 20 percent more likely than non-whites to engage in illicit activities, such as "skipping school, use of alcohol and marijuana, vandalism, shoplifting, drug dealing, robbery, assault, and gambling" (Levine and Rubinstein 2013).

As Jordan Weissmann, a journalist who writes about the economy for *The Atlantic*, contends,

> One of the great privileges that comes with being born wealthy, white, and male in the United States of America is that you can get away with certain youthful indiscretions . . . if you're an upper-middle-class Caucasian, chances are the cops aren't going to randomly stop and frisk you in the street under dubiously constitutional pretenses. And if you do somehow get caught, . . . your parents can likely afford a decent lawyer to help plea bargain your way into some light community service.
>
> (Weissmann 2013: 1)

This important research reveals that white middle class men enjoy advantages that support their entrepreneurship. More significantly, it indicates that the very characteristics that foster successful enterprise—risk-taking and challenging authority—may result in negative life consequences for non-whites to a greater extent than for white middle class youth. For example, there is substantial evidence of black/white disparities in juvenile justice outcomes. Ira Schwartz, a policy analyst, stated that "minority youth accounted for more than half of juveniles in custody despite research showing that they did not disproportionately commit crimes," suggesting that selection bias and racial discrimination contributed to racial disparities in the use of confinement (quoted in Davis and Sorensen 2013). Weissmann (2013) concludes, "to be successful at running your own company, you need a personality type that society is a lot more forgiving of if you're white."

Racial, class, and gender differences in enterprise are exacerbated by class position and immigrant status; American entrepreneurs are not a homogenous group but have a variety of intersectional identities. Human capital, social capital, and the context of reception combine to shape different entrepreneurial outcomes among men and women, the working and middle classes, and racial and ethnic minorities, with privileged white middle class men outperforming their white female and ethnic and racial minority counterparts. Nevertheless, all entrepreneurs, regardless of gender, class, or race, strive to achieve the American Dream. These entrepreneurs do not lack the ambition, drive, passion, or "entrepreneurial spirit," to succeed in business ownership; many, however, lack the resources that support business ownership, economic mobility, and longevity. These unequal outcomes are rooted in the social stratification of the American economy, which shapes different trajectories of entrepreneurial success across race, class, and gender.

DISCUSSION QUESTIONS

1. The idea that entrepreneurs come from all walks of life is not always supported by the numbers. What do the trends tell us about group differences in

entrepreneurship? How do race, class, and gender shape entrepreneurial differences among men and women, the middle and working classes, and Blacks and Whites? How does the intersection of these categories shape entrepreneurial outcomes?

2. The United States dominates other industrialized nations in the number, diversity, and enthusiasm of its entrepreneurs. What are some social and cultural factors that might explain this phenomenon?

3. Although entrepreneurs often start their businesses to "make money" or "be their own boss," others decide to go into business for non-economic reasons. What are some of the social reasons entrepreneurs go into business? Are there differences across race, class, and gender?

IV: Joe the Plumber and the Myth of New Small Businesses as "Job Creators"

❧⤢❧

"We are going to fight for Joe, my friends, we are going to fight for him."
John McCain

In 2008, Samuel Joe Wurzelbacher, a.k.a. "Joe the Plumber," became a national figure after approaching Democratic presidential candidate Barack Obama on the campaign trail to ask, "Do you believe in the American Dream?" Wurzelbacher explained that he planned to eventually take over the plumbing business where he was employed, moving from worker to entrepreneur. But he was hesitant to make this investment, he claimed, because he worried about the liability he might incur under Obama's tax plan as a business owner making over $250,000. At the time of his question, Wurzelbacher was unlicensed, had no available resources to purchase the business, and his yearly income at the time was far less than half the $250,000 sum he worried about. Yet John McCain, the Republican nominee, embraced "Joe the Plumber" as an "entrepreneur" whose business would suffer from the policies of Senator Barack Obama if he were elected president.

Throughout the remainder of the campaign, "Joe the Plumber" came to symbolize the American middle class and personify would-be entrepreneurs striving to achieve the American Dream. National attention to "Joe the Plumber" was so great that his plight took center stage at the third and final debate between Senators McCain and Obama, who together mentioned his name twenty-six times.

At a campaign rally in Philadelphia the day after the debate, McCain shouted, "Joe's the man! He won, and small businesses won across America." At another rally in Florida, McCain said, "Joe's dream is the American Dream to own a small business that will create jobs, and the attacks on him are an attack on small businesses all over this nation." In response, Barack Obama and his vice-presidential running mate Joe Biden began to quip, "How many plumbers do you know making $250,000?" Biden backed up his point with factual evidence, stating that 98 percent of small businesses had a taxable income of below $250,000. He and Senator Obama left another incorrect assumption unchallenged, however: the widespread and seemingly common sense belief that small businesses "create jobs."

The Myth of Small Businesses as Job Creators

In the second sentence of the 2014 State of the Union address, President Obama emphasized the importance of America's entrepreneurs to the U.S. economy in general and to the creation of jobs in particular. He stated, "Today in America . . . an entrepreneur flipped on the lights in her tech start-up and did her part to add to the more than eight million new jobs our businesses have created over the past four years." The president's WhiteHouse.gov website highlighted this claim as well, noting that "small businesses are the engines of job creation and essential to strengthening our national economy." The president is not alone in embracing **small businesses**, which are defined by the federal government as firms with fewer than 500 employees, as crucial to economic growth. Politicians from both sides of the aisle, news media outlets, CEOs, policy makers, analysts, and academics regularly repeat the notion that small businesses drive the American economy.

This assumption is supported by empirical data. For example, the Bureau of Labor Statistics observed that between 1993 and 2013, small businesses contributed 63 percent of new jobs in the United States, or fourteen million of the twenty-three million jobs created during this period (SBA 2014). Similarly, a study by the Small Business Administration (SBA) concluded that, on balance, small businesses provided a "greater share of new jobs" than large businesses (i.e., firms with 500 employees or more) (Headd 2010: 3). Of the six million small and large firms that reported one or more employees in 2012:

> 90 percent have fewer than 20 employees, a relatively small number of employer firms (less than 10 percent) have 20–400 employees, and relatively fewer employer firms (0.3 percent) have 500 employees or more. Employer firms with fewer than 20 employees provide about 18 percent of all jobs, employer firms with 20–499 employees provide about 31 percent of all jobs, and employer firms with 500 or more employees provide about 51 percent of all jobs. Overall, employer firms with fewer than 500 employees provide almost half (49 percent) of all jobs.
>
> (2013: 2–3)

The finding that small businesses provided slightly less than half of all jobs in the United States supports the idea that small businesses are the engine of the economy thanks to their contributions to job creation in the American labor market. Read differently, however, these findings reveal that the vast majority of firms (99.7 percent) are designated as small businesses. This observation calls into question the role that size plays in job creation. Is it possible that small businesses create more jobs only because there are so many more small businesses than large ones?

Studies aimed at identifying the specific characteristics of firms that facilitate job creation challenge the popular perception that "smaller is better." Against conventional wisdom, these studies suggest that it is not the size of the business that matters for job creation but rather its age. Younger and newer firms that have been open for less than one year, known as **start-ups**, are beginning to replace small businesses as the presumptive key to new job creation. Contemporary research reveals that younger and newer firms matter because they "add jobs to the economy in their founding year and, for the most part, are not old enough to eliminate them yet." In support of this claim, the Kaufmann Foundation recently reported that, "of the overall 12 million new jobs added in 2007, young firms were responsible for the creation of nearly 8 million of those jobs."

In light of this new direction in research, the assumption that small businesses are synonymous with job creation appears to be more of a myth than a reality as age seems to trump size as the driver of new jobs. Still, researchers do not yet fully understand when and how start-ups create new jobs, and some even suspect that start-ups' contributions have been overstated. After all, a third of new businesses close within one year and half close within two years. Additionally, a report from Cornell University acknowledged that start-ups have an immediate impact on employee hiring but nevertheless concede this less-than-optimistic conclusion about the role of start-ups in net job creation or economic development:

> In sum, the positive effect of start-ups on net job creation diminshes over time because 'most businesses start small, stay small, and close just a few years after opening.' [In fact], from 2005 through 2010, start-ups created 19.6 million jobs and non-start-ups destroyed approximately 23.1 million jobs, for a net change in employment of minus 3.4 million jobs.
>
> (2013: 10)

Likewise, the most recent data collected by the SBA on employer firm births and deaths reveals that "10 to 12 percent of firms with employees open each year and about 10 to 12 percent close" each year. Findings suggest that these contrasting events effectively cancel each other out in terms of net job creation (see Table 4.1).

In many ways, the latest research on the role of start-ups in job creation mirrors previous research on small business. This research casts doubt on the role of start-

Table 4.1 Employer Firm Births and Deaths, 2012

	2000	*2009*	*2010*	*2011*
Births	481,985	410,038	389,774	409,040
Deaths	407,947	508,668	446,944	470,736

Note: Figures are from March to March.
Source: U.S. Census Bureau, Birth and Death Statistics.

ups as net job creators, especially within a larger context of firm births and deaths. Taken together, recent studies on both small businesses and start-ups pose a serious challenge to the conventional wisdom that entrepreneurs starting new small businesses are always "job creators" and that the businesses they start are the "engines of the economy." The mythology surrounding small startups in the United States has contributed to their pride of place in American life. Insofar as this myth highlights the benefits of entrepreneurial activity to the American economy and celebrates innovators and entrepreneurs who are striving to achieve the American Dream, it is harmless. But its strong and persistent influence on economic and governmental policy is troubling. Policy prescriptions and government programs designed to support small business creation development as a strategy to address economic stagnation or decline are based on a faulty premise. A better approach to facilitate job creation would be to set aside the myth, instead asking the question, "what types of businesses facilitate job creation and spur economic growth?"

Mice, Gazelles, and Elephants

Recent research by economist David Birch draws our attention to a segment of the business sector shown to stimulate job creation: "high impact" firms called "**gazelles**" (Birch 1979; Birch and Medoff 1994). In an online article for *INC* entitled "Who Really Creates the Jobs?" Burlingham (2012) writes how Birch changed his thinking that "smaller is always better" in terms of job creation:

'Gazelles' is a term Birch coined to describe the small percentage of companies that accounted for virtually all the net job growth he had observed in his research. As such, the concept represented a significant shift in his thinking. In an interview many years later, he said that he needed 'a simple, almost naïve way of explaining what was going on in the economy.' His solution was a business taxonomy consisting of **elephants**, **mice**, and **gazelles**. 'The big companies, elephants, [like Amazon and Wal-Mart] are slow and not very innovative,' he said. 'Then there are a large number of very small firms—mice—that run around but fail to develop. And then the gazelles . . . [are] small firms that grow quickly and create employment.'

(2012)

According to the SBA, gazelles are identified by sales and employment measures. In particular, gazelles are firms that consistently double their sales over a four-year period (Acs et al. 2009). Joshua Zubrun, a national economics correspondent for the Wall Street Journal, suggests that when it comes to job creation, neither firm size nor age matters. Instead, the essential characteristic that produces new jobs is a firm's rate of expansion. This trait sets gazelles apart from mice and elephants. These companies are sometimes associated with the high-tech industry, but this is not always the case. For example, recently celebrated gazelles include firms like Twitter and Facebook as well as smaller firms in the service and health care industries. The SBA in 2013 reports that gazelles:

- account for nearly all employment growth in the economy;
- come in all sizes;
- exist in all regions, all states, and all counties;
- tend to be located in metropolitan areas and within twenty miles of a central business district;
- exist in nearly all industries; and
- on average, are smaller and younger than other businesses, but "the average high-impact business is not a start-up and has been in operation for about 25 years."

(2013: 10)

Importantly, gazelles comprise only a very small fraction of the American business sector. As Zumbrun (2009) writes, "unsurprisingly, gazelles are rare creatures . . . [A] mere 2 to 3 percent of all companies [in 2008] were high-impact firms." According to the SBA, 350,000 gazelle firms were responsible for creating 10.7 million jobs. This contribution to job creation is remarkable, especially in comparison to non-impact firms, which "shed, on average 4.1 million jobs" over the same period.

To illustrate gazelle firms' rapid expansion, the SBA profiled Allied Reliability, an engineering services firm located in Charleston, South Carolina:

By all measures, Allied Reliability is representative of America's high impact companies. Consider its story: In 1997, John Schultz and John Langhorne formed Allied Services Group. Mr. Schultz brought to the company more than seven years of experience and product knowledge as a reliability engineering manager at Eli Lilly. Mr. Langhorne brought to the company 23 years of operations management experience and knowledge. For the first two years, Mr. Schultz traveled the U.S. building awareness of the company while Mr. Langhorne implemented the operational components of the business. In 1999, the partners landed their first major contract with Cargill, one of the nation's largest producers and marketers of food, agricultural, financial, and industrial products and services. From 2000 to 2004, the company focused on hiring qualified employees and developing its service lines. By 2007, the company had more than 100 employees and rebranded itself as Allied Reliability to better reflect its growing service offerings. In true high impact company style, from 2008 to 2010 the company further expanded its operations both domestically and internationally during the worst economic climate since the Great Depression. Today, Allied Reliability has 300 employees in ten countries and its annualized revenue is growing at a staggering 30 percent.

(2011: 55–56)

Like Allied Reliability, gazelle firms are characterized by a rapid rate of expansion, business owners' high human capital attainment, and the ability to easily secure capital to establish the business.

Though high impact firms make significant contributions to job creation as they expand, these contributions are generally limited. Gazelles' fast-growth period rarely lasts longer than three or four years and is seldom repeated. High impact firms that display back-to-back periods of job creation are exceedingly rare, making up roughly 2 percent of the total population of high impact firms. Coad and colleagues (2014: 106) thus argue that much remains to be learned about gazelle firms, including whether they are "superior" or "struggling"; whether they are "flimsy" with respect to net job creation; and importantly, whether they have the potential for "sustained high growth" or if, as others suggest, their rapid rise is followed by a "fast decline."

Making up less than 1 percent of the American business sector, **elephants** are even rarer than gazelles, typically defined as large companies that employ 500 or more people. Conventional wisdom on the role of elephants in job creation is uncontroversial: elephants are not associated with positive net job creation. In fact, they are generally characterized as "job destroyers." For example, multiple studies have found that when the quintessential elephant—a new Walmart store—opens, retail employment in the local geographic area drops precipitously (Geier 2013; Hicks 2009). One study investigating the effects of new Walmarts across 3,000 counties finds that with each new store, Walmart "kills an average 150 retail jobs at the county level, with each Walmart worker replacing about 1.4 retail workers." Research shows that elephant firms destroy jobs because they squeeze suppliers to cut labor costs in order to provide lower prices. In addition, the lower prices elephants offer cannot be matched by mom and pop stores, which are put out of business. Finally, large corporations are prone to cut jobs in response to a weak economy or to technological improvements requiring fewer workers to maintain productivity and profit.

That said, large corporations still contribute markedly to the American labor market. After all, nearly half of the American workforce is employed by elephant firms. Moreover, large firms account for 57 percent of total compensation to American employees. On balance, however, large corporations are job destroyers in the sense that once they become wildly profitable, they maintain their status by cutting labor costs, which often means cutting jobs. These cuts then neutralize the gains in net job growth made by small businesses and start-ups, although they may not completely cancel out the jobs created by gazelles.

Mice is the metaphorical name given to **microbusinesses**, which are typically defined as small businesses with four employees or fewer and which include **non-employer firms**, or businesses with no paid employees. Non-employer firms are rarely included in the discussion of job creation because by definition, they operate without employees. These businesses involve **self-employed** owners who work on their own account and may or may not rely on the unpaid labor of one or more family members. *Remarkably, of the almost twenty-eight million firms in the United States today, twenty-two million (79 percent) report no employees on their payroll.* When non-employer firms are combined with the smallest of the employer firms (those with four employees or less), these microbusinesses account for 95 percent of the total businesses in the United States.

Because 95 percent of American businesses are microbusinesses, or mice, the overwhelming majority of U.S. businesses are dismissed from any real discussion of job creation. But when this relationship is examined from the perspective of the business owners, mice firms may in fact have a significant impact. Reimagining "jobs" to include those provided for the business owners themselves reveals that mice firms make a substantial contribution to job creation. As Light and Roach (1996: 193) remind us, for some groups, such as necessity entrepreneurs, business ownership is a "survival strategy" or "economic lifeboat"—a last-ditch alternative to unemployment in the general labor market. A report by the Global Entrepreneurship Monitor published in 2013 indicates that entrepreneurship in the United States is motivated by necessity to a greater degree than in the past several years; in fact, "21 percent of U.S. entrepreneurs started their businesses because they had no other options for work; this compares to 18.5 percent on average for the developed economies" (Global Entrepreneurship Monitor 2013: 22).

Moreover, mice firms are disproportionately owned by non-white minorities and women, groups that face unequal outcomes in employment due to discrimination in the labor market. Specifically, a higher percentage of black (97.5 percent) and Latino (95 percent) owned businesses are microbusinesses as compared to businesses owned by whites (89.9 percent) and Asians (88.3 percent). Although a slightly higher proportion of Asians than whites own businesses with more than four employees, white-owned microbusinesses report higher sales returns than their Asian counterparts or other minority groups. With respect to gender, women are more likely to own microbusinesses than men (94.7 percent and 88.4 percent, respectively). Finally, the U.S. Census reports that when mice firms hire employees, they are more likely than larger employer firms to hire minorities and women. Taken together, these numbers suggest that mice firms are particularly important for the employment opportunities of disadvantaged owners and workers. These results demonstrate a need to bring microbusiness into the discussion of job creation, especially as it corresponds to job creation among the self-employed, minorities, and women.

Conclusion

This chapter exposes the myths associated with American entrepreneurship and job creation. Against traditional thought, this chapter reveals that small businesses and start-ups do not drive the economy through job creation. In fact, only one rare breed of firms demonstrate a unique capacity to create new jobs. Known as gazelles, these firms are characterized by a rapid rate of expansion. However, even gazelle firms' contributions to net job growth appear to be short-lived and unsustainable. In contrast, elephant firms, which are large corporate firms employing more than 500 people, make up the smallest share of the American business sector, smaller even than that of gazelles (1 percent and 2–4 percent, respectively); however, elephants are job destroyers, not job creators. Finally, microbusinesses known as mice are often dismissed from job creation, even as they provide jobs to a significant segment of the entrepreneurial class—the self-employed. Mice firms also contribute markedly to job creation among disadvantaged groups, including racial minorities and women.

The "Joe the Plumbers" of America can and should be recognized for striving to achieve the American Dream; however, their supposed contribution of jobs to the American economy is little more than a myth. Ultimately, the real job creators comprise a select, small, and elite group of highly educated and monied entrepreneurs who own high-impact firms on the one hand and disadvantaged self-employed workers on the other.

DISCUSSION QUESTIONS

1. Search online newspapers and articles on entrepreneurship and "job creation" or entrepreneurs as "job creators." What is the general consensus of these

online resources regarding these relationships? This chapter offers an alternate perspective. Why do you think this chapter's conclusion differs from the mainstream American viewpoint?

2. The chapter suggests that some types of businesses create jobs and some types of businesses do not. On balance, do most businesses create jobs or not? Do you think there are differences across race, class, and gender, in the types of businesses that create jobs? Explain.

3. "Joe the Plumber" became a national figure during the 2008 presidential election. Given what you know about the relationship between entrepreneurs and the economy, how do you explain the effort exerted by two presidential candidates, the press, and the media, to interview and respond to Joe the Plumber's concerns?

V: The False-Positive Claim

Recessions Stimulate Entrepreneurship

～～～☓～～

It is a well-known fact that recessions, commonly defined as two consecutive quarters of decline in gross domestic product (GDP), hurt the economy.[1] Recessions are marked by an economic slowdown or slump as observed by declining incomes, production, sales, and employment. According to the National Bureau of Economic Research (NBER), the latest recession began in December of 2007 and ended in June of 2009. This recession, which lasted eighteen months, was the longest downturn on record in the United States since World War II. During this period, the Bureau of Labor Statistics reported that unemployment doubled from 5 percent to 10 percent. The effects of the recession touched the lives of many Americans. A 2010 survey conducted by the Pew Research Center (2010: i) found that half of American adults experienced "a spell of unemployment, a cut in pay, a reduction in hours or [became] involuntary part-time workers." Moreover, foreclosures brought about by the twin forces of high unemployment and negative equity due to dropping home prices reached a peak that was "twice as high as during any other recession in recent history," as over three million families lost their homes during this period (Cooley and Rupert 2010).

But just as every cloud has a silver-lining, popular belief suggests that recessions are good or even "fabulous" for entrepreneurship. There are several reasons why recessions are thought to stimulate and strengthen entrepreneurship, including a forced business dynamism that leads to innovation and, at times, wildly successful businesses. General Electric, General Motors, MTV, Microsoft, and FedEx are just a few prosperous companies that got their start during recessions. According to Joseph Schumpeter (1942), a German economist and political scientist considered to be one of the most prominent scholar in the area of entrepreneurship, recessions foster periods of "creative destruction," a hallmark of entrepreneurship under capitalism, which captures the "churning" of businesses as new and innovative businesses replace older and outdated ones. From this point of view, recessions are thought to have a cleansing or purifying effect by destroying weak or unhealthy companies and reigning in unrealistic market speculation and, in the process, stimulating new economic growth and job creation. As researchers at the Global Entrepreneurship Monitor contend, "entrepreneurship is thought to be one of the mechanisms that helps turn around recessions by reallocating resources in such a way that promising new activities replace obsolete economic activities."

Robert Fairlie, an economist at the Kaufmann Foundation, used data from the Current Population Survey to examine the effects of the recession on entrepreneurial activity. He posited that the recession might have a positive or negative effect on entrepreneurship; after all, the Great Recession was associated with an increase in housing foreclosures, which meant that fewer people could use their homes as collateral to start a business. Moreover, businesses that were just breaking even before the crisis may have closed or filed bankruptcy in the wake of the sluggish economy. On the other hand, the Great Recession resulted in eight million unemployed workers with few alternatives for employment who may have felt pushed into entrepreneurship. His analysis revealed evidence that the recession increased foreclosures and shuttered weaker businesses, which likely dampened entrepreneurial activity. Nevertheless, he concluded that the staggering unemployment rate sparked a net increase in business creation overall. This finding confirmed the Kaufmann Foundation's claim that despite the recession, "the number of people reporting entry into entrepreneurial activity in the United States reached its highest point over the last fourteen years (Kauffman 2010: 2)."

There are several reasons why recessions are thought to foster entrepreneurial activity. First, recessions create a "buyer's market," whereby "opportunity entrepreneurs" may capitalize on cheap and plentiful low or high-skilled labor, less competition, and increased efficiencies to gain a foothold in or expand their businesses. Recessions are also associated with a rise in necessity entrepreneurs, sometimes called "accidental entrepreneurs." This latter group is generally comprised of individuals who are motivated to start their own businesses due to pending job losses. An important but nuanced difference between these two categories is that opportunity entrepreneurs are presumed to retain some decision-making capacity or choice in their pursuit of entrepreneurship; they are often characterized as high-skilled professionals who seek out business opportunities to exploit, but who, in the absence of such opportunities, would be well-compensated in the labor market. In contrast, necessity entrepreneurs are best described as having no choice but to start a business in the face of recent unemployment or persistent underemployment. Beyond differences in motivation, these categories are associated with divergent economic outcomes. Opportunity entrepreneurs are typically characterized as the key to economic recovery. Accidental entrepreneurs are sometimes discussed in those terms, especially when associated with laid-off professional or managerial workers who were driven to pursue business ownership as a means to maintain the high salaries associated with their prerecession careers. In contrast, the "necessity" label is almost exclusively used to describe low-skilled or "hard to employ" workers that turn to self-employment as a last recourse. Necessity entrepreneurs are, on average, less educated, more racially diverse, and make less money than opportunity or accidental entrepreneurs and, often, earn less than their similarly skilled, wage-working counterparts.

Accidental Entrepreneurs in an Economic Downturn

> "Like a pack of velociraptors among a herd of herbivores, accidental entrepreneurs are quick to react and take advantage of changing conditions, which gives them an edge over their larger competition."
>
> David Ribeiro, Partner Account Manager at
> Symantec 2012, Entrepreneur

The quote above captures the "survival of the fittest" rhetoric associated with accidental entrepreneurs during the Great Recession. Media reports and newspaper outlets from the Wall Street Journal to the New York Times celebrated the idea that accidental entrepreneurs were thriving in spite of the recession. A study of accidental entrepreneurs commissioned by Symantec Corporation found, that unlike traditional entrepreneurs who start their businesses to "be their own boss," accidental entrepreneurs were "agile, highly educated, tech-savvy and battle-tested business professionals" driven by "profits not passion." Accidental entrepreneurs share some characteristics in common, which set them apart from prerecession entrepreneurs:

- More than one-third of the founders of postrecession companies came from a position with a large (500+) employee company.
- Thirty-five percent left their large employers due to the recession.
- They are optimistic about growth. Half of them expect to double their number of employees and increase their revenue by at least 10 percent (http://investor. symantec.com/investor-relations/press-releases/press-release-details/2012/ Symantec-Finds-Accidental-Entrepreneurs-Leverage-Scalable-Technology-to-Fast-Track-Growth/default.aspx).

As Scott Shane, professor of entrepreneurial studies at Case Western Reserve University, noted, even Robert Reich, former U.S. Labor Secretary, embraced the idea, stating, "[2009] was a fabulous one for entrepreneurs . . . even exceeding the number of start-ups during the peak 1999–2000 technology boom."

Nevertheless a closer look at the numbers or more accurately, different numbers, calls into question the positive relationship between the Great Recession and entrepreneurship. It appears that the positive trend that is often recounted is based on a false-positive of sorts, whereby data is reported that suggests a condition that does not actually exist. While it is true that many laid-off workers started their own businesses in larger numbers during the Great Recession than before or after the recession, it was also the case that a greater number of these new and more established businesses failed during this heightened period of economic uncertainty overall.

The Recession Increased Business Entry, but Not Enough to Offset Business Exit

Shane (2010) offers a corrective to the traditional view that recessions help entrepreneurs. He contends that such findings are based on partial data only; specifically, the percentage of the working-age population who *starts* a business. According to that measure, from 2007 to 2009 the number of people who entered into business, "rose from 300 people per 100,000 to 340 per 100,000"—a fourteen-year high. In contrast, the Bureau of Labor Statistics (BLS) reported a 6 percent decline in entrepreneurs during that same period. Shane explains that the difference in entrepreneurial activity between these data sources is rooted in the failure of researchers to consider and report on the number of people who also exit business ownership. After all, the net or overall total number of business owners is not captured by statistics on entry alone.

A reconsideration of the presumed positive relationship between recessions and enterprise is important for several reasons. First, it provides a counteractive to the notion that starting a business is a reasonable strategy of economic absorption for unemployed persons. Accidental entrepreneurs may include high-skilled professionals who want to maintain their middle class lifestyle and for which business owner-ship may lead to economic progress; however, many "necessity" entrepreneurs who turned to self-employment during the recession were unemployed or under-employed before the start of the recession. These "hard to employ" low-skilled, often minority or immigrant workers engage in survival self-employment as a "last ditch" effort to find work. Don José's story, profiled in my previous research, illustrates the experiences of necessity entrepreneurs (Valdez 2011: 48).

Don José: A Necessity Entrepreneur

As an undocumented, Spanish-speaking Mexican immigrant with a grade-school education, don José was relegated to work in the low-skilled, low-wage construction industry. He started his restaurant, *Café Taco*, located in Little Mexico in 1977, when he could no longer meet the physical demands of his job (as a roofer). After painstakingly saving $4,000 over several years, don José turned to three Mexican men in his community who were known to lend money at an inflated rate of interest. He borrowed $5,500 from these semi-formal lenders and with the modest sum of $9,500 he started his own business. As an entrepreneur, however, his earnings have not improved (his income continues to fall below the poverty line as it did when he was employed as a roofer). He explains,

> I couldn't make much sometimes [but] I'm still alive. I provided for my family. I never had to go asking for food stamps or anything, thank God . . . For someone who has studies and education that's nothing, but for me it's a lot. For an educated person, it doesn't take long to move up, because they have computers and they can click here and there and everywhere. I on the other hand look at a computer and I don't know where to click. That's the problem for the person who doesn't have an education, it's very hard, it's pure work, work, work.

Remarkably, don José played the lottery and won in 1987, which allowed him to pay off his medical bills for diabetes and heart disease (it goes without saying that he did not have health insurance) and some of his other debts, including the loan he received from co-ethnics. If not for the lottery winnings, don José is convinced that his restaurant would have closed, as it was often the case that the business did not generate enough income to break even.

Don José is not the picture that comes to mind when thinking about the American entrepreneur. His entrepreneurial activity, which was triggered by necessity, is not the type that tends to increase during recessions, nor is it associated with the form of enterprise that sparks a turnaround in the economy. Nevertheless, this form of entrepreneurial activity has been on the rise since the end of the Great Recession.

According to the Global Economic Monitor, necessity entrepreneurs increased their ranks by a fifth of all entrepreneurs, from 12 percent in 2008 to a high of 28 percent. Although this group does not feature prominently in stories of successful accidental entrepreneurs, it is notable that African Americans, a group with, on average, lower aggregate levels of education and work experience when compared to whites or most other racial groups, were the group most likely to engage in start-up self-employment during the recession. The increase in black entrepreneurship suggests a rise in necessity entrepreneurs during recessions, a group that is even less likely to survive and thrive than their opportunity counterparts.

The Future of Entrepreneurship Looks . . . Uncertain

The current rate of new entrepreneurial activity in the United States reflects a decrease from that reported during the recession. A recent Kauffman foundation brief noted that, "the rate of business creation declined from 300 out of 100,000 adults in 2012 to 280 out of 100,000 adults in 2013." This decline was observed for the working-age population and across all demographic groups, including the U.S.-born and foreign-born, men and women, young and old, and members of all ethnic and racial minority groups including Latinos and non-Hispanic whites.

Conspicuously, today's lower rate of start-up entrepreneurial activity matches that reported prior to the Great Recession of 2008. This trend is in keeping with previous research that posited an inverse relationship between entrepreneurship and the strength of the economy. Specifically, a strong labor market is associated with a decrease in new entrepreneurial activity, whereas a weak labor market is associated with an increase in new entrepreneurial activity. Consistent with this relationship, the proportion of accidental and necessity entrepreneurs decreased during a period of economic recovery in 2013 from that reported in 2008. On the other hand, "opportunity entrepreneurs," or those who pursue entrepreneurship to capitalize on opportunities for growth or economic mobility, are on the rise. The recent shift in entrepreneurial activity from necessity or accidental entrepreneurs during the recession to opportunity entrepreneurs postrecession suggests that the economy and labor market are recovering from the economic downturn. This conclusion is supported by a recent Kauffman Foundation report, which stated,

> The decline in business creation over the past year is likely due to improved labor market conditions, putting less pressure on individuals to start businesses out of necessity. Trends in the share of business starts, presented in this report for the first time, indicate that the share of new entrepreneurs who are not coming directly out of unemployment was much higher in 2013 than the share at the end of the Great Recession.
>
> (2013: 2)

In other words, the labor market of today is strong enough to keep working-age Americans employed and out of "accidental" or "necessity" business ownership.

From this perspective, the future of entrepreneurial activity in the United States should not be expected to increase over time, as it appears to be related to the cyclical nature of the economy. However, recent indications suggest that the U.S. economy is not returning to "business as usual" following the recession. In a recently released report by the Brookings Institution, economists Ian Hathaway and Robert E. Litan (2014) contend that American **business dynamism** is on a path of unprecedented decline. Business dynamism is defined as the process by which "more productive firms drive out less productive ones, new entrants disrupt incumbents, and workers are better matched with firms (2014: 1)." Using data from the U.S. Census Bureau and Business Dynamics Statistics, they find a steady increase in business deaths, across all regions and in all industries, which has not been met with a similar increase in business births. In fact, as of 2006, the level of business deaths that they observe exceed the level of births for the first time since this data were collected (thirty-plus years). The report does not provide a clear explanation for the declining trends of business dynamism and entrepreneurship beyond acknowledging that older and larger businesses, what are referred to as **elephants**, are outperforming newer and smaller businesses, including **gazelles** (see Chapter IV for a discussion of elephants, gazelles, and mice). Along with business consolidation, other factors that may be at play include changing demographics (older entrepreneurs are not being replaced by younger entrepreneurs) and increased global competition.

Secular Stagnation and Declining Business Dynamism

According to Lawrence Summers (2014), an economist and former treasury secretary for the Clinton Administration, the United States is in a once-in-an-era state of stagnation, "in which sluggish growth, output and employment at levels well below potential, and problematically low real interest rates might coincide for quite some time." Regarding entrepreneurship, "secular stagnation" is characterized by a decline in innovation, business dynamism, and fewer young firms. In a study from the University of Maryland, researchers posited that the most important factor that contributed to the decline in young firms was business consolidation, whereby "mom and pop stores have increasingly given way to big box stores like Walmart and Target." Additionally, high-tech firms that have the potential to generate transformative or new industries are also on the decline. These twin forces have resulted in a serious decline in business dynamism. According to a study by the Brookings Institution, "The shifting age composition [that is the decline in younger firms] accounts for 32 percent of the observed decline in job creation, 20 percent of the decline in job destruction and 26 percent of the decline in job allocation . . ."

The troubling decline in business dynamism suggests that the older and larger the business, the better off the business is, whereas the younger the firm, the more vulnerable the business is. Hathaway and Litan (2014), the authors of the Brookings report conclude, "it appears to have become increasingly advantageous to be an incumbent, particularly a mature one, and increasingly disadvantageous to be a new entrant in the American economy." Under such conditions, entrepreneurial activity is fundamentally stunted:

> . . . consider the need for new products and services in a country full of concentrated industries. When a company had dozens of potential competitors in various geographic regions, there was an incentive to innovate before the

other guy does. In a concentrated market, competitors are few, and growth may come more from mergers and government lobbying than new product lines. For entrepreneurs, why start something new in such an environment? The current tech boom might serve as a counterexample, but consider that for most venture-backed companies, the ultimate exit plan is for sale of the firm to an existing behemoth, not continued independent operations.

(Garland 2014)

This state of affairs is complicated further by the consolidation of particular areas of the economy that promote entrepreneurship, like the financial sector. As Richard Florida, a senior editor at *The Atlantic*, noted, "The U.S. financial services sector went from 13,000 independent banks to half that number, while the top ten banks grew from 20% market share to 60%. As of 2013, the top ten banks had 70% of the market." In this environment of increasing business consolidation and decreasing dynamism, fewer opportunities for entrepreneurial activity exist and fewer would-be entrepreneurs are prepared to take on the added risk and competition.

Conclusion

There is no doubt that the United States remains the most entrepreneurial advanced economy in the world, in spite of persistent economic uncertainty. Nevertheless, this chapter concludes that during economic downturns like the Great Recession, American entrepreneurship declines overall. This claim goes against orthodox economic thought, which suggests that recessions spur entrepreneurial growth and activity. Although these statements are seemingly at odds, there is a compelling explanation to reject the generally accepted false-positive claim that recessions are good for enterprise: first, most of the entrepreneurial activity in the United States is due to start-up activity; second, a "persistently high" percentage of entrepreneurs are necessity entrepreneurs; third, start-up activity by necessity entrepreneurs reaches its highest peak during recessions; fourth, and consequently, these fragile and vulnerable businesses die at a higher rate than nonrecession, nonnecessity start-ups.

The rate of nascent entrepreneurial activity is captured by the Global Entrepreneurship Monitor's measure, the **Total Early Stage Entrepreneurial Activity Rate (TEA)**. The TEA rate is much higher in the United States than in other developed countries. For example, in 2012, the average level of nascent activity in the United States was double that of other countries (9 percent compared to 4.4 percent). Likewise, the United States reported a higher percentage of necessity entrepreneurs than other developed countries, regardless of the strength of the economy. For example, in 2013 when the economy was on the rebound, 21 percent of all U.S. entrepreneurs indicated that they started their businesses due to necessity, compared to 19 percent of entrepreneurs outside the U.S.

Fundamentally, the relationship between recessions and entrepreneurship is more complicated and less positive than the conventional wisdom suggests. Although the United States remains a country of high entrepreneurship whether the economy is strong or weak, nascent businesses owned by necessity or accidental entrepreneurs are more likely to develop during periods of economic decline. They are also more likely to fail because many do not have the resources required or the experience needed to withstand the uncertainty and hardship that arises during recessions, which include a decline in consumer demand, a decrease in investment capital, and less access to credit from banks or suppliers in related industries. Coupled with the closure of more established businesses during such periods, the overall picture suggests that net entrepreneurship declines during recessions. Finally, recent studies suggest that structural forces complicate an individual's drive or ambition to start a business. In particular, business dynamism, or the churning brought on by the emergence of new businesses and the destruction of older ones, which sparks economic growth, is experiencing a significant downward trend. American business dynamism generally follows a circular trend that maps onto the strength of the economy. Yet it has not recovered following the recent economic downturn; instead, it has been on a steady decline for the last three decades, and especially since 2006. If this trend is not reversed, perhaps with policies that promote or accelerate business development and opportunities, it is likely that entrepreneurial activity in the United States will continue to decline as larger and more established businesses that can withstand market uncertainty and competition consolidate smaller and younger enterprises.

DISCUSSION QUESTIONS

1. Orthodox economic thought suggests that during periods of economic uncertainty, like the Great Recession, entrepreneurship increases. It suggests further that entrepreneurial activity has the potential to turnaround recessions and stimulate growth. Why is this traditional understanding flawed?
2. An old adage states, "Statistics can be made to prove anything." What does this chapter reveal about the use of statistics?
3. Imagine that you are working during a recession, and your boss tells you that you will be laid off in six weeks. What would you do: look for another job or start your own business? Explain your reasoning.
4. Conduct an online search to find three successful businesses that started during the Great Recession. What do these businesses have in common? Would you consider the entrepreneur who started each business a necessity, accidental,

or opportunity entrepreneur? Do you think these different designations matter for their eventual success?

5. This chapter closes with some evidence of an uncertain future with respect to entrepreneurship. How is the decline in business dynamism related to a decline in entrepreneurship and a decline in job creation? What are some of the larger structural forces that may be contributing to the U.S. decline in entrepreneurship? What are some possible solutions that government, public policy makers, and private corporations might develop to combat the decline?

Note

1. According to the National Bureau of Economic Research (NBER) a recession is

    a significant decline in economic activity spread across the economy, lasting more than a few months, normally visible in real GDP, real income, employment, industrial production, and wholesale-retail sales. A recession begins when the economy reaches a peak of activity and ends when the economy reaches its trough. Between trough and peak, the economy is in an expansion.

    For more information, see the latest announcement from the NBER's Business Cycle Dating Committee, dated 9/20/10. www.nber.org/cycles/dec2008.pdf

VI: Conclusion

✙

Against the American Dream ideology that through hard work and determination anyone can own a successful business in the United States, this book introduces an intersectional approach to American enterprise. In so doing, it demonstrates how race, class, gender, and other social group formations, combine to shape the entrepreneurial outcomes of diverse groups. Moreover, this book offers a reconsideration of the notion that American entrepreneurs are either "rugged individualists" or "collectivist" ethnic entrepreneurs; it also challenges the strongly held American belief that entrepreneurs who work hard will always be successful, and that entrepreneurial activity improves the larger economy and society. By considering the intersections of race, class, and gender, within the context of the highly stratified U.S. economy, this book reveals how agency among individuals and groups, and structural forces in the economy, combine to shape, transform, and reproduce the divergent life chances of American entrepreneurs, and condition their potential to achieve the American Dream through enterprise.

Moreover, and against the traditional and strongly held belief that American entrepreneurship is the "engine of the economy" that "creates jobs" and can turnaround a sluggish or depressed economy, this book shows that for the most part, entrepreneurial activity in the United States achieves more modest outcomes. Entrepreneurship is overwhelmingly a non-employer enterprise in America; it provides most business owners (approximately 80 percent) with an alternative to unemployment or underemployment in the general labor market, or perhaps, allows some entrepreneurs to forego wage-work in favor of the nonpecuniary benefits that self-employment provides, namely, a sense of autonomy and independence. As such, American enterprise is not strongly associated with job creation nor has it sparked an economic recovery following the latest Great Recession. In fact, the recent economic downturn has been associated with an era of stagnation and a decline in business dynamism, whereby small business ownership and entrepreneurial activity is giving way to business consolidation—in other words, bigger and older businesses are swallowing up newer and more vulnerable start-ups.

Nevertheless, the U.S. government continues to suggest that entrepreneurship is associated with economic growth and remains focused on ensuring that "small businesses are poised to start, grow, and create jobs." In 2012, President Obama declared November "National Entrepreneurship Month" and November 6 "National Entrepreneurs' Day." On the White House webpage, the U.S. Office of Management and Budget outlines a budget that prioritizes small business creation. Likewise, the Small Business Administration's (SBA's) proposed budget plans to generate $16 billion in small business loans to operate and expand and provide lines of credit, to build on the existing seventeen tax cuts that are available to small businesses, and to increase tax credits to encourage business start-ups. Moreover, the Affordable Care Act (ACA), also known as "ObamaCare," includes stipulations that provide subsidies and breaks to small business owners who provide health care to their employees. The Obama administration also proposes to increase investment in economically distressed regions to promote businesses in underserved markets. Finally, the SBA is further poised to offer "angel investor" funds to secure funding for "innovative" companies. These policies and proposals aim to facilitate small businesses in the current period, but such policies are nothing new in the United States. From the establishment of the Reconstruction Finance Corporation (RFC) in 1932 by President Hoover, a response to businesses that were hurt by the effects of the Great Depression, to what is known today as the SBA established in 1953, the federal government has been involved in programs to build entrepreneurship and businesses in the United States, and has always linked business development with economic progress and prosperity.

Clearly the U.S. government is committed to fostering entrepreneurship, regardless of the actual relationship between entrepreneurial activity and economic progress. Most Americans agree with pro-business policy prescriptions, which tend to serve their own interests, as national surveys consistently show that most Americans dream of starting their own business one day. This book, however, suggests that the presumed benefits of entrepreneurial activity in the United States may be overstated—instead, it demonstrates that significant economic progress is generally constrained to a privileged few—those would-be entrepreneurs with access to substantial economic and social resources and support (i.e., predominately, white, middle class, men), and those few elite companies with high-growth potential, coined "gazelles." These observations call into question public and government policy aimed at promoting entrepreneurs and their businesses. After all, most start-ups fail, and most businesses do not create jobs. As the Bureau of Labor Statistics reports, *"About half of all new establishments survive five years or more and about one-third survive 10 years or more. As one would expect, the probability of survival increases with a firm's age. Survival rates have changed little over time."*

A recent study argues that public policy makers should stop encouraging Americans to start their own businesses. That study contends that "typical startups" do not spark economic growth or create jobs, so the government should "stop subsidizing the formation of the typical start-up" and instead, "focus on the subset of businesses with growth potential (Shane 2009: 145)." The study's author, Scott Shane, proposes instead that policy makers should start thinking "like venture capitalists and concentrate time and money on extraordinary entrepreneurs, and worry less about the typical ones (146)." He concludes that policy makers should reduce incentives in order to dissuade Americans from starting businesses in the first place. There may be some merit in the call to dismantle programs that create start-up businesses that are doomed to fail. It is possible to imagine a different set of policies that would strengthen the economy; for example, an economic policy that redirected funds earmarked for small business formation toward programs that provide job training or public works, would certainly improve the economic conditions of would-be necessity entrepreneurs, who instead could remain employed in well-paying government jobs. Investing in American workers by providing greater job security, health care, and opportunities for advancement, through a federal jobs program, would likely decrease the number of "necessity" or "accidental" entrepreneurs who start businesses in order to avoid unemployment in an uncertain economy.

Despite that, policy makers and government officials alike remain committed to promoting business ownership. After all, the American Dream of owning one's own business is part of the fabric of American society. And as this book shows, there are good reasons for the government to continue to promote and encourage entrepreneurship in the United States, even if most business startups do not create jobs or drive the engine of the economy. First, startups provide jobs for the unemployed and underemployed, including necessity and accidental entrepreneurs. In the absence of a safety net for disadvantaged workers, self-employment provides an avenue of economic integration for vulnerable populations and the hard-to-hire. Second, there is substantial evidence that a few "high growth" start-ups do in fact create jobs. By providing opportunities for would-be entrepreneurs to start businesses, especially those with innovative ideas but without access to sufficient start-up capital, the government may sponsor a successful high-growth company. Third, the end of the Great Recession has been followed by a "secular stagnation," characterized by a significant decline in business dynamism and an increase in business consolidation. Promoting new enterprise through policy may foster entrepreneurial activity among those would-be entrepreneurs who might otherwise wait for better market conditions, which may help spark a more robust economic recovery. Finally, opportunities for business start-up should be encouraged from diverse groups and diverse companies, to increase the potential for the development of innovative and creative enterprises among ethnic and racial minorities and women, who are less likely to start enterprises or succeed in business.

Ultimately, this book reveals that the American Dream of business ownership and economic success is only possible for a few. At the same time, entrepreneurship appears to provide a crucial and viable alternative to joblessness or market uncertainty, exploitation and discrimination based on race, ethnicity, gender, and other social group formations, and blocked mobility in the formal and informal labor markets due to racism or sexism. This comprehensive and systematic examination of entrepreneurship sets the stage for a serious reconsideration of the promise and pitfalls of business ownership, and the relationship between American entrepreneurship and the American Dream.

DISCUSSION QUESTIONS

1. Do you think public policy should promote small business and entrepreneurship? Why or why not? What types of government policies would help foster successful entrepreneurship?
2. This book has presented evidence suggesting that entrepreneurship does not always result in achieving the American Dream. What is your definition of the American Dream? Do you believe that entrepreneurship can lead to the American Dream?
3. A thought experiment: imagine a new company that has the potential to become a high-impact, job-creating Gazelle. Create a business plan that would detail the conditions of development. What would it take to start such a company? How much investment capital would be required to launch your business? What would the company produce or sell? What are the top five reasons your company would succeed?

Bibliography

Acs, Zoltan J., William Parsons and Spencer Tracy. (2008). "High Impact Firms: Gazelles Revisited," Office of Advocacy, the United States Small Business Administration http://www.massmac.org/newsline/0902/high_impact_firms.pdf (accessed May 1, 2015).

Amoros, Jose Ernesto and Niels Bosma. (2014). "Global Entrepreneurship Monitor 2013 Global Report: Fifteen Years of Assessing Entrepreneurship Across the Globe," Universidad del Desarrollo and Global Entrepreneurship Research Association (GERA).

Baron, Robert A. and Scott A. Shane. (2007). *Entrepreneurship: A Process Perspective,* 2nd edition. Mason, OH: Thomson South-Western.

Birch, David L. (1979). *The Job Generation Process.* Cambridge, MA: MIT program on neighborhood and regional change, Massachusetts Institute of Technology.

Birch, David L. and James Medoff. (1994). "Gazelles." In *Labor Markets, Employment Policy and Job Creation,* 159–167.

Browne, Irene and Joya Misra. (2003). "The Intersection of Gender and Race in the Labor Market," *Annual Review of Sociology* 29(1):487–513.

Burlingham, Bo. (2012). INC. Who Really Creates the Jobs? www.inc.com/magazine/201209/bo-burlingham/who-really-creates-the-jobs.html (accessed May 1, 2015).

Coad, Alex, Sven-Olov Daunfeldt, Werner Holzl, Dan Johansson and Paul Nightingale. (2014). "High-growth firms: Introduction to the special section," *Industrial and Corporate Change.* 23(1):91–112.

Collins, Patricia Hill. (1990). *Black Feminist Thought: Knowledge, Consciousness, and the Politics of Empowerment.* Boston, MA: UnwinHyman.

Conley, Dalton and Miriam Ryvicker. (2005). "The price of female headship: Gender, inheritance, and wealth accumulation in the United States," *Journal of Income Distribution.* 13(3/4):41–56.

Cooley, Thomas F. and Peter Rupert. (2010). "The Great Housing Recession Continues," Forbes. www.forbes.com/2010/04/20/housing-foreclosure-unemployment-opinions-columnists-thomas-cooley-peter-rupert.html (accessed May 1, 2015).

Davis, Jaya and Jon R. Sorensen. (2013) "Disproportionate minority confinement of juveniles. A national examination of black–white disparity in placements, 1997–2006," *Crime & Delinquency.* 59(1):115–139.

De-Masi, Paul. (2004). "Defining Entreprneurship," Financing Microenterprises Report. www.gdrc.org/icm/micro/define-micro.html. (accessed August 17, 2015).

Digler, Robert J. (2013). "Small Business Administration and Job Creation," Cornell University ILR School. http://digitalcommons.ilr.cornell.edu/key_workplace/1014/?utm_source=digital

commons.ilr.cornell.edu%2Fkey_workplace%2F1014&utm_medium=PDF&utm_campaign =PDFCoverPages (accessed May 15, 2015).

Eisenmann, Thomas. (2013). "Entrepreneurship: A Working Definition," Thomas R. Eisenmann. Harvard Business Review. https://hbr.org/2013/01/what-is-entrepreneurship (accessed May 17, 2015).

Europa. (2015). "Definition of Micro, Small and Medium-Sized Enterprises," Europa: Summaries of EU Legislation: Business Environment. http://europa.eu/legislation_summaries/enterprise/ business_environment/n26026_en.htm (accessed May 15, 2015).

Fairlie, Robert W. (2010). "Kaufmann Index of Entrepreneurial Activity Report". www.kauffman. org/~/media/kauffman_org/research%20reports%20and%20covers/2010/05/kiea_2010_ report.pdf (accessed May 1, 2015).

Fairlie, Robert W. (2013). "Kauffman Index of Entrepreneurial Activity, 1996–2012," Ewing Marion Kauffman Foundation, Kansas City, MS. Monitor, Global Entrepreneurship. GEM 2013 Global Report. http://gemconsortium. org/docs (accessed May 18, 2015).

Fairlie, Robert W. and Alicia M. Robb. (2007). "Why are Black-owned businesses less successful than White-owned businesses? The role of families, inheritances, and business human capital," *Journal of Labor Economics*. 25(2):289–323.

Fairlie, Robert W. and Alicia M. Robb. (2008). *Race and Entrepreneurial Success: Black-, Asian-, and White-Owned Businesses in the United States*. Cambridge, MA: Massachusetts Institute of Technology Press.

Fairlie, Robert W. and Alicia M. Robb. (2009). "Gender Differences in Business Performance: Evidence from the Characteristics of Business Owners Survey," Small Business Economics 33(1): 375–395.

Fenn, Donna. (2013). "Unselfconsciously Sexy Style," INC. May 28. www.inc.com/30under30/ donna-fenn/nasty-gal-sophia-amoruso-2013.html (accessed August 17, 2015).

Garland, Eric. (2014). "Why America Is Losing Its Entrepreneurial Edge," Harvard Business Review. https://hbr.org/2014/05/why-america-is-losing-its-entrepreneurial-edge/ (accessed May 23, 2015).

Geier, Kathleen. (2013). "Walmart's Big Lie: No, it Doesn't Create Jobs!" Salon. August 5. www.salon.com/2013/08/05/walmart%E2%80%99s_big_lie_no_it_doesnt_create_jobs/ (accessed May 23, 2015).

Georgellis, Yannis, John Sessions and Nikolaos Tsitsianis. (2007). "Pecuniary and non-pecuniary aspects of self-employment survival," *The Quarterly Review of Economics and Finance*. 47(1):94–112.

Global Entrepreneurship Monitor. (2012). "Total Early Stage Entrepreneurial Activity Rate (TEA)," www.gemconsortium.org/about/news (accessed May 1, 2015).

Hathaway, Ian and Robert E. Litan. (2014). "Declining Business Dynamism in the United States: A Look at States and Metros," Economic Studies at Brookings Institution. www.brookings. edu/~/media/research/files/papers/2014/05/declining%20business%20dynamism%20litan/ declining_business_dynamism_hathaway_litan.pdf (accessed May 23, 2015).

Headd, Brian. (2010). "An Analysis of Small Business and Jobs," U.S. Small Business Administration, Office of Advocacy, March 2010, http://archive.sba.gov/advo/research/rs359tot.pdf (accessed May 15, 2015).

Hicks, Michael J. (2009). "Estimating Wal-Mart's impacts in Maryland: A test of identification strategies and endogeneity tests," *Eastern Economic Journal*. 34(1):56–73.

Hondagneu-Sotelo, Pierrette. (2001). *Domestica: Immigrant Workers Cleaning and Caring in the Shadows of Affluence*. Berkeley, CA: University of California Press.

Johnson, Steve A., David A. Schauer and Dennis L. Soden. (2002). "Analysis of small business lending in Texas," *IPED Technical Reports*. 18.

Kauffman Foundation. (2010). "Kaufmann Index of Entrepreneurial Activity," Kauffman Foundation. www.kauffman.org/~/media/kauffman_org/research%20reports%20and%20covers/2014/04/kiea_2010_report.pdf (accessed May 1, 2015).

Kilby, Peter. (1971). *Entrepreneurship and Economic Development*. New York, NY: Free Press.

Kilby, Peter. (2003). "The Heffalump Revisited," Journal of International Entrepreneurship, 1(1):13–29.

Levine, Ross and Yona Rubinstein. (2013). "Smart and Illicit: Who Becomes an Entrepreneur and Do They Earn More?" NBER Working Paper No. 19276. www.nber.org/papers/w19276 (accessed May 5, 2015).

Light, Ivan Hubert. (1972). *Ethnic Enterprise in America: Business and Welfare Among Chinese, Japanese, and Blacks*. Berkeley, CA: University of California Press.

Light, Ivan Hubert and Edna Roach. (1996). Self-Employment: Mobility Ladder or Economic Lifeboat? In *Ethnic Los Angeles*, Roger Waldinger and Mehdi Bozorgmehr, Eds., 193–214. New York: Russell Sage.

Morin, Rich. (2010). "One Recession, Two Americas," Pew Research Center Social and Demographic Trends. www.pewsocialtrends.org/2010/09/24/one-recession-two-americas/ (accessed August 17, 2015).

Obama, Barak. (2014). State of the Union Address. Office of the Press Secretary. The White House. www.whitehouse.gov/the-press-office/2014/01/28/president-barack-obamas-state-union-address (accessed May 1, 2015).

Office of Advocacy, U.S. Small Business Administration, March to March, Employer Firm Births and Deaths Statistics (BDS). (2007). https:/www.sba.gov/sites/default/files/FAQ_sept_2012 (accessed May 1, 2015).

Oliver, Melvin and Thomas M. Shapiro. (1995). *Black Wealth/White Wealth: A New Perspective on Racial Inequality*. New York: Routledge.

Pager, Devah and Hana Shepherd. (2008). "The sociology of discrimination: Racial discrimination in employment, housing, credit, and consumer markets," *Annual Review of Sociology*. 34:181–209.

Portes, Alejandro and Ruben G. Rumbaut. (2006). *Immigrant America: A Portrait*. Berkeley, CA: University of California Press.

Ribiero, David. (2012). "Born from the Flames," Entrepreneur. www.entrepreneurmag.co.za/advice/doing-business-in-sa/business-landscape/born-from-the-flames/ (accessed May 1, 2015).

Robb, Alicia M. (2002). "Entrepreneurial performance by women and minorities: The case of new firms," *Journal of Developmental Entrepreneurship*. 7(4).

Robb, Alicia M. and Robert W. Fairlie. (2006). "Tracing Access to Financial Capital Among African-Americans from the Entrepreneurial Venture to the Established Business," Conference Proceedings, Research Conference on Entrepreneurship Among Minorities and Women.

Sarachek, Bernard. (1978). "American entrepreneurs and the horatio alger myth," *The Journal of Economic History*. 38(2):439–456.

Schumpeter, Joseph A. (1934). *The Theory of Economic Development: An Inquiry into Profits, Capital, Credit, Interest and the Business Cycle*. New Brunswick, NJ: Transaction Publishers.

Schumpeter, Joseph A. (1942). *Capitalism, Socialism, and Democracy*. New York: Harper & Brothers.

Schwartz, Seth, Jennifer Unger, Elma Lorenzo-Blanco, Sabrina Des Rosiers and Associates. (2014). "Perceived context of reception among recent hispanic immigrants: conceptualization, instrument development, and preliminary validation." *Cultural Diversity and Ethnic Minority Psychology*. 20(1):1–15.

Shane, Scott. (2009). "Why encouraging more people to become entrepreneurs is bad public policy," *Small Business Economics*. 33:141–149.

Shane, Scott. (2010). "Contrary to What You May Have Read, the Recession Hasn't Been Good for Entrepreneurs," Small Business Trends. http://smallbiztrends.com/2010/06/recession-not-good-for-entrepreneurs.html (accessed May 23, 2015).

Small Business Administration. (2014). Office of Advocacy. Frequently Asked Questions. www.sba.gov/sites/default/files/FAQ_March_2014_0.pdf (accessed May 1, 2015).

Summers, Lawrence. (2014). "Washington must not settle for secular stagnation," Financial Times. Published January 5, 2014. www.ft.com/intl/cms/s/2/ba0f1386-7169-11e3-8f92-00144feabdc0.html#axzz3j5oMEMlC (accessed August 17, 2015).

Swansburg, John. (2014). "The Self-Made Man: The Story of America's Most Pliable, Pernicious, Irrepressible Myth," Slate, September 29. www.slate.com/articles/news_and_politics/history/2014/09/the_self_made_man_history_of_a_myth_from_ben_franklin_to_andrew_carnegie.html (accessed May 5, 2015).

Tracy, Spencer L. Jr. (2011). "Accelerating Job Creation in America: The Promise of High-Impact Companies," Small Business Administration, Office of Advocacy. Corporate Research Board. Washington, DC 20037. www.sba.gov/sites/default/files/HighImpactReport.pdf (accessed May 1, 2015).

U.S. Census Bureau. (2007). "2007 Survey of Business Owners." www.census.gov/econ/sbo/07menu.html (accessed May 17, 2015).

U.S. Census Bureau. (2012). Employer and Nonemployer Statistics. www.census.gov/econ/nonemployer/index.html (accessed May 1, 2015).

Valdez, Zulema. (2008). "The effect of social capital on white, Korean, Mexican and black business owners' earnings in the US," *Journal of Ethnic and Migration Studies*. 34(6):955–973.

Valdez, Zulema. (2011). *The New Entrepreneurs: How Race, Class, and Gender Shape American Enterprise*. Palo Alto, CA: Stanford University Press.

Valenzuela, Abel. Jr. (2001). "Day labourers as entrepreneurs?" *Journal of Ethnic and Migration Studies*. 27(2):335–352.

Vallejo, Jody Agius and Jennifer Lee. (2009). "Brown picket fences. The immigrant narrative and 'giving back' among the Mexican-origin middle class," *Ethnicities*. 9(1):5–31.

Warren, Tracey, Karen Rowlingson and Claire Whyley. (2001). "Female finances: Gender wage gaps and gender assets gaps," *Work, Employment and Society*. 15(3):465–488.

Weissmann, Jordan. "Entrepreneurship: The Ultimate White Privilege?" The Atlantic, published August 16, 2013. www.theatlantic.com/business/archive/2013/08/entrepreneur ship-the-ultimate-white-privilege/278727/ (accessed August 17, 2015).

Wronski, Mike. (2013). "The 10 Differences Between Entrepreneur and Employees," www.mikewronski.co.za/2013/01/09/the-10-differences-between-entrepreneurs-and-employees/ (accessed May 17, 2015).

Xavier, Siri Roland, Donna Kelly, Jacqui Kew, Mike Herrington, and Arne Vorderwulbecke. (2013). "Global Entrepreneurship Monitor 2012 Report," Universidad del Desarrollo and Global Entrepreneurship Research Association (GERA).

Zissimopoulos, Julie and Lynn A. Karoly. (2007). "Transitions to self-employment at older ages: The role of wealth, health, health insurance and other factors," *Labour Economics, Elsevier*. 14(2):269–295.

Zumbrun, Joshua. (2009). "Hunting for Gazelles," Forbes. www.forbes.com/forbes/2009/1116/careers-small-businesses-unemployment-hunting-for-gazelles.html (accessed August 17, 2015).

Glossary

Business Dynamism: A process by which newer and more productive firms drive out less productive and older firms; the churning of businesses

Context of Reception: The social and economic opportunity structure of a society as well as the degree of openness versus hostility among members of the society. Schwartz and colleagues (2014: 1) contend that

> . . . in a positive context of reception immigrants are welcomed and can pursue the American Dream (i.e., find jobs and develop supportive social ties). In a negative context of reception immigrants are isolated, have difficulty finding jobs, and experience discrimination or perceive hostility.

Elephant: Large company that employs 500 or more people

Entrepreneur: A person who starts a business or enterprise

Entrepreneurial Capital: The experiences and skills relevant to business ownership that promote attitudes and values that facilitate business ownership, such as working in the family-owned business

Entrepreneurship: The process of developing or starting a business or enterprise

False-Positive: Data that suggests a condition that does not actually exist

Gazelle: High-impact firms that consistently double their sales over a four-year period

Human Capital: An individual's combined educational attainment and work experience

Institutional Racism: Discrimination that takes place within the larger social context, disadvantages that are associated with social stratification

Mice: Microbusiness, typically defined as a small business with between one and four employees

Self-Employed: Business owner who works on his/her own account

Small Business: The SBA defines a small business using a combination of measures including employee size, industry classification, and average receipts, which generally includes manufacturing businesses with less than 500 employees.

Social Capital: Access to resources based on group membership and relationships

Social Stratification: A system of unequal distribution of power, wealth, and status in a hierarchically-ranked society

Start-up: A newly created company or business in the first stage of operations, usually open for less than one year

Statistical discrimination: Using an ascribed characteristic of an individual, such as their racial group membership, to make inferences about their abilities or capacities, based on beliefs about the group (i.e. stereotypes)

Total Early Stage Entrepreneurial Activity (TEA): Global Entrepreneurship Monitor measure of nascent entrepreneurial activity

Index

For Product Safety Concerns and Information please contact our EU
representative GPSR@taylorandfrancis.com
Taylor & Francis Verlag GmbH, Kaufingerstraße 24, 80331 München, Germany